*Simple Wisdom*
*for*
*Challenging Times*

# Simple Wisdom for Challenging Times

Thoughts and questions to help you live
a happier, more meaningful life

Copyright©2003 by Gail Van Kleeck

Published by Abundance Enterprises
PO Box 201, Westwood, Ma. 02090

Orders @ www.simplewisdom.com or 781-255-0808

Editorial:
Cover Design:  Accent Press, Dedham, MA
Graphic Design:  Accent Press, Dedham, MA

**Library of Congress Cataloging-in-Publication Data**
Van Kleeck, Gail.
    Simple wisdom for challenging times / Gail Van Kleeck
    p. cm.
    ISBN 0-9745523-0-5

    1. Conduct of life.   I. Title.

BF637.C5V36 2003        813'.54
                      QBI33-1648

Printed in Canada

# Simple Wisdom
## for
# Challenging Times

Gail Van Kleeck

An Abundance Enterprises Publication
*Books that make a difference*

*For my children Kim and Ken*
*and for their children*
*Taylor, Amber, Connor and Skyler.*
*May you always have dreams that you are*
*willing to work for.*

# Introduction

*Since we serve others best when we touch their lives with our own sense of well being and happiness, in today's world it is increasingly essential that we learn to become more personally happy and fulfilled.*

*Each of us has a choice about how we respond to the everyday challenges of life. Our response to these challenges is important because it is contagious. It affects not only the quality of our own lives, but the quality of the lives of those around us.*

*When we respond with compassion and a sense of possibility, we carry the healing feelings of hopefulness and gratitude within us as we go out into the world. When we respond with anger and judgment, we carry the destructive feelings of frustration and resentment within us. Because this is so, each of us has a responsibility to look more carefully at how we are living our individual lives.*

*This collection of simple thoughts and questions is dedicated to everyone who wishes to build a firmer foundation for a fuller and happier life. The more positive and purposeful our personal lives become the more we participate in creating a world that reflects the best in each of us.*

# Table of Contents

*Page XV*
*Reader's Guideline*

## *A*

*Page 1*
*Abundance, Abuse, Acceptance, Accomplishment, Action,
Affirmation, Allowing, Aloneness, Alternatives, Anger,
Answers, Appreciation, Asking For What We Need,
Assumptions, Authenticity, Awareness*

## *B*

*Page 21*
*Balance, Being Enough, Being Loved, Beliefs, Blame,
Blessings, Boundaries, Busyness*

## *C*

*Page 31*
*Caring For Others, Celebrating Our Uniqueness, Change,
Choice, Clarity, Communication, Compassion, Compromise,
Connection, Contribution, Control, Courage, Creativity*

# D

*Page 47*

*Deadlines, Death, Decisions, Declaration Of Our
Potential For Happiness, Denial, Depression,
Disappointment, Dishonesty, Dreams*


# E

*Page 59*

*Earning Love, Effort and Effortlessness,
Empty Spaces, Expectation*


# F

*Page 65*

*Failure, Fairness, Faith, Fear, Fixing, Focus,
Forgiveness, Freedom From Within, Frenzy, Fun, Future*


# G

*Page 79*

*Gentleness, Getting Through, Giving, Goals,
God's Plan, Gratitude, Guilt*


# H

*Page 89*

*Happiness, Helplessness, Holding On, Honesty,
Hope, Humanity, Humility, Humor*

# I

Page 99
Independence, Inner Child, Inner Voice,
Inspiration, Integrity, Interdependence

# J

Page 107
Journal Keeping, The Journey, Joy, Judgment

# K

Page 113
Kindness, Knowledge

# L

Page 117
Lack, Learning, Letting Go, Limitations,
Limitlessness, Listening, Living, Loose Ends,
Loneliness, Love

# M

Page 131
Making A Difference, Martyrdom, Meaning Well,
Memories, Mission Impossible,
Our Mission, Mistakes, Moments, Money,
Mothers and Daughters

# N

*Page 145*
*Needing, Neediness, Needs, Negativity,*
*Niceness, Not About us, Noticing, Now*


# O

*Page 155*
*Opportunity, Optimism, Feeling Overwhelmed*


# P

*Page 161*
*Pain, Parenting, The Past, The Path, Payment,*
*Peace, Perception, Perfection, Persistence, Perspective,*
*Pieces, The Plan, Playfulness, Possibility, Power From*
*Within, The Present, Priorities, Prison, Procrastination,*
*Progress, Promises, Proving*


# Q

*Page 187*
*Quality, The Quest, Questions*


# R

*Page 193*
*Reality, Receiving, Regrets, Rejoicing, Relationships,*
*Rescuing, Resentment, Responsibility, Risk, Rules, Ruts*

# S

Page 207
Safety, The Secret, Seeds, Self-Absorption, Self-Appreciation,
Self-Awareness, Self-Caring, Self- Celebration,
Self-Empowerment, Self-Gratitude, Selfishness,
Self-Knowing, Self-Love, Self- Protection, Self-Worth,
Stress, Struggle, Success, Supporting Others, Survivorship


# T

Page 231
Time, Today, Trust, Truth


# U

Page 237
Understanding, Uniqueness, Feeling Useful,
Using What We Have


# V

Page 243
Values, Vantage Point, Velcro®, Being A Victim,
Vision, Vulnerability

# W

*Page 251*
*Wholeness, Wisdom, Wishing, Wonder, Work, Writing*


# XY Z

*Page 259*
*X Marks The Spot, Being 'Xactly Where We Need To Be,*
*Yes, Yet, Zest,*

*Acknowledgements* ...................................... *266*

*About Gail Van Kleeck* .............................. *269*

*Other Work By Gail Van Kleeck* .................. *271*

*To Order Gail's Books* ................................. *272*

# Reader's Guideline

*Simple Wisdom for Challenging Times is a collection of thoughts and observations to help you explore the many ways you can personally participate in creating a fuller, more rewarding and happier life. Since participation is an essential part of any exploration, you will need to ignore the rules you once learned in childhood about never writing in books. You'll want to read this one with a pen in your hand.*

*You can use your pen to jot down thoughts and feelings, to record memories or experiences as they come to you or to add insights or observations of your own.*

*While there is a place for notes at the end of each section, there is plenty of room on each page for you to comment as you go along. Feel free to turn down page corners or to use stickers, tabs or ribbons to mark thoughts that you'd like to return to. While you can complete the open-ended questions in writing, you may choose instead to simply think about them as you go about your day.*

*The more tattered, dog-eared and personal this book becomes, the more it is likely to help you create a fuller, happier and more personally rewarding life.*

*Abundance, Abuse,*
*Acceptance, Accomplishment,*
*Action, Affirmation, Allowing,*
*Aloneness, Alternatives,*
*Anger, Answers, Appreciation,*
*Asking For What We Need,*
*Assumptions, Authenticity,*
*Awareness*

# Abundance

If we seek abundance and celebrate it as it comes to us, it becomes more clearly present in our lives.

It's difficult to create a sense of abundance if we're continually dragging our memory of past lack into every thought we have about the future.

The decision to actively participate in creating our abundance empowers and enriches every facet of our lives.

*How would you complete these phrases about abundance?*

*What is presently abundant in my life is___*
*A memory of lack I could choose to set aside is__*
*I could participate in creating greater abundance by___*

## *Abuse*

Sometimes we're too forgiving and too willing to bend to someone else's needs. Sometimes we're too willing to be the one who hurts because we believe we can handle the hurting. All too often our desire to be overly loving and understanding causes us to feel disrespected, taken for granted and emotionally abused. Could it be that by our example, we actually teach others that abusive, thoughtless, behavior is acceptable?

Whenever we criticize someone without an accompanying attempt to understand or acknowledge them, we ourselves may be guilty of abuse.

*How would you complete these phrases about abuse?*

*I can teach others to treat me more respectfully by____*
*I need to be less critical of____*

# Acceptance

The quality of our relationships is shaped by our willingness to accept and honor even those things we don't fully understand.

If we're overly critical of ourselves, we're not very likely to be accepting of others.

One good thing about how our eyesight changes as we grow older is that we don't see life's flaws quite so clearly.

*How would you complete these phrases about acceptance?*

*A place in my life I could be more accepting is___*
*I am too critical of myself about___*
*Lately, I've noticed I'm more accepting of___*

# Accomplishment

Honoring ourselves for who we are, as well as for what we do, is an essential part of life's work. It's far too easy to slip into that place where we value our days based on how much we can cram into them.

What sort of difference might it make in our lives if we honored moments filled with awareness as much as we honor moments filled with accomplishment?

It's important not to confuse what we accomplish with who we are.

*How would you complete these phrases about accomplishment?*

*Something I like about myself is___*
*I'm grateful for my awareness of___*
*Sometimes my focus on accomplishments keeps me from___*

# *A*

*Take.* **Action.** *Do something q day to achieve goals.*

Deciding to take some sort of action, even when the outcome isn't completely clear, helps us feel more powerful. It also saves us from the self doubting that is so much a part of inaction.

The more we pay attention to the many successful actions we've already taken, the easier it becomes to build on them.

Focusing on the consistent, small steps we can take to reach our goals is much more empowering than focusing on how much farther we still need to go.

·‿·‿·‿·‿·‿·

*How would you complete these phrases about taking action?*

*An action I once took
that made me feel more confident was___
Some of my most successful actions have been___
A small step I could take today is___*

# A

## Affirmation *What I hope for is possible.*

"I would like to have this or better." What an amazing thought! Whenever we hope for something, we need to remind ourselves that the outcome could be even richer and more rewarding than our limited sense of knowing is able to imagine.

The more we affirm that what we need in life is possible, the more we begin to see that it truly is.

Imagine what might happen if we promised ourselves to begin each day thinking of just one more reason to feel grateful.

*How would you complete these phrases about affirmation?*

*A time when the outcome*
*was better than I'd imagined was___*
*A positive thought I could carry with me today is___*
*Some things for which I'm already grateful are___*

# Allowing

When we put our energy into allowing and
encouraging, rather than into forcing and
demanding, we create a more peaceful and
fulfilling life.

Sometimes our task is to simply set life's table,
then to stand back and allow others to choose
the food they wish to eat.

*How would you complete these phrases about allowing?*

*Someone I need to encourage more often is____*
*For me allowing means____*

# *Aloneness*

We often see our connection with others more
clearly when we are in the depth of our own
life's lonely, sometimes searching stream.


Perhaps it is in the times of our aloneness that
we create a space for life's music to play within us.


Whenever we protect our vulnerability by keeping
others from knowing how much we need them,
we contribute to our own aloneness.


*How would you complete these phrases about aloneness?*

*Someone with whom I feel truly connected is___*
*When I am alone___*
*Someone I need more than I am willing to admit is___*

# Alternatives

The more we focus on the possibility of alternatives, the more of them we are likely to see.

Respectful relationships are usually built on a willingness to seek and explore alternatives.

The more we look for alternatives the less we find to fear.

*How would you complete these phrases about alternatives?*

*When I think about the possibility of alternatives
I notice that\_\_\_
Someone with whom I need to explore alternatives is\_\_\_
I could expand my search for alternatives by\_\_\_*

## *Anger*

Diffuse anger shuts out communication just like fog shuts out the world around us. While the possibility for communication is always present, the anger we are carrying makes it difficult to see.

Clearly focused anger is a powerful tool. It helps us set the kinds of boundaries that keep our spirits safe.

It's interesting how appropriately expressed anger empowers us in a way that feeling sorry for ourselves never does.

*How would you complete these phrases about anger?*

*My diffuse anger is blocking my communication with\_\_\_*
*My clearly focused anger*
*could help me set better boundaries about\_\_\_*
*I could use my anger more appropriately by\_\_\_*

# Answers

There is rarely a fully right or wrong answer. What's right for us can be clearly wrong for someone else. What's right for us now can also change as we gather more information and experience. The more we accept the seeming inconsistencies of life the happier we are likely to be.

Our stubborn belief in the rightness of our answers keeps us from asking the kinds of questions that could enrich and expand our lives.

*How would you complete these phrases about answers?*

*I accept the inconsistencies of life more easily when____
A question I need to ask myself is____*

# *Appreciation*

Learning to look for the things we appreciate
in others is an essential step toward building
relationships that are more loving, more
powerful and more mutually respectful.

When we are drawing the perfect picture of
what we would like our lives to hold, we need
to leave room to appreciate what is and to stay
aware of the powerful possibilities that lie
beyond our perfect picture's frame.

Without some level of appreciation for what
our lives hold now, there can be little true feeling
of joyful expectation for what is about to be.

*How would you complete these phrases about appreciation?*

*Some of the qualities I appreciate in others are___*
*A time that was better than I'd imagined was___*
*Some of the things I appreciate today are___*

## *Asking For What We Need*

While pretending to be more self-reliant than we actually feel can protect our vulnerability, sometimes it keeps us from asking for the things we truly need.

One of the secrets for getting what we need more often, is to be sure that the person we are asking truly has what we are needing.

The clearer we are about what we need and the more we practice asking, the more likely we are to receive it.

*How would you complete these phrases about asking for what we need?*

*Something I've been pretending not to need is___*
*Someone I trust to be there for me is___*
*Something I could ask for today is___*

## *Assumptions*

Assumptions close the door on true communication.

The best phrase to get us beyond our habit of assuming is, "Tell me about it."

The more we truly listen, the less we are likely to assume.

*How would you complete these phrases about assumptions?*

*A time I kept the door open to communication was___*
*A time when something changed because I listened was___*
*I listen better when___*

# Authenticity

Being loved for who we are is not very likely to happen if we're pretending to be someone or something we are not.

While being true to ourselves can cost a great deal, when we're untrue to ourselves the price usually escalates.

We can't fit ourselves into someone else's picture of who we should be without risking the loss of what is real and authentic for us.

*How would you complete these phrases about authenticity?*

*Someone with whom I can be my true self is____*
*I could become more true to myself by____*
*The price I pay for not being authentic is____*

# *Awareness*

We might not need to search so hard for life's gifts if we were more aware of the times they simply come to us.

So much that gives life meaning lies within our minds. If we pay attention to the thoughts that bring us happiness and hope, we can teach ourselves to choose those kinds of thoughts more often.

Sometimes it's possible that we contribute to our own pain. How can we walk around with our eyes half-open and expect to avoid the sharp edges of life?

*How would you complete these phrases about awareness?*

*Some gifts of life I didn't need to work for are____*
*Some thoughts that bring me a sense of hope are____*
*When I pay more attention to my own instincts I ____*

## *Personal Notes*

Abundance_____

_____

_____

Abuse_____

_____

_____

Acceptance_____

_____

_____

Accomplishment_____

_____

_____

Action_____

_____

_____

Affirmation_____

_____

_____

Allowing_____

_____

_____

## *Personal Notes*

Aloneness_____

_____

_____

Alternatives_____

_____

_____

Anger_____

_____

_____

Answers_____

_____

_____

Appreciation_____

_____

_____

Asking For What We Need_____

_____

_____

Assumptions_____

_____

_____

## *Personal Notes*

Authenticity_____

_____

_____

Awareness_____

_____

_____

*Balance, Being Enough,*
*Being Loved,*
*Beliefs, Blame, Blessings,*
*Boundaries, Busyness*

## *Balance*

Life is not about juggling, although sometimes we act as though it is. Life is about balance and about the choices we make to create and maintain it.

Why is it that we see the negative parts of who we are and what we do so much more clearly than the positive? How much better our lives might be if we could learn to look at ourselves through more balanced and compassionate eyes.

Whenever we feel needy, unappreciated and out of balance, we've probably said "yes" just a little too often.

*How would you complete these phrases about balance?*

*I could create better balance in my life by\_\_\_*
*Seeing myself through more compassionate eyes would\_\_\_*
*I could teach myself to say yes less often by\_\_\_*

## *Being Enough*

Our most sabotaging belief is the belief that we are somehow not enough.

The sun doesn't shine all the time, yet despite its inconsistency, we still honor it as a source of warmth and light. Although we may not consistently be all we would like to be, we still need to honor the many times when we are truly and fully enough.

*How would you complete these phrases about being enough?*

*Believing that I'm not enough keeps me from____*
*Some of my more consistent positive attributes are____*

## *Being Loved*

Being lovingly supported by others requires us to act respectfully towards ourselves.

To give up who we are in exchange for being loved is never a very good bargain.

*How would you complete these phrases about being loved?*

*I act disrespectfully towards myself when I___*
*When I am authentic enough to be loved*
*for who I really am I___*

# Beliefs

If we don't believe that life has gifts to give us,
how can we truly expect to receive them?


We can't change our lives until we change our
behavior. We can't change our behavior until
we change the way we see. We can't change the
way we see until we change what we believe.


If we believe we can teach ourselves to live
happier, more empowering lives, our unleashed
inner spirits will help us find the way.

* * * * *

*How would you complete these phrases about beliefs?*

*Some of the gifts I have already received are____*
*One of my beliefs that limits me is____*
*I could live a happier, more empowering life by____*

# *Blame*

Blaming keeps us from exploring our choices
and from understanding that genuine happiness
ultimately depends upon us.


The more we blame others for what happens in
our lives, the more we see ourselves as victims.


The more we blame others for what happens in
our lives, the less we are able to change it.


*How would you complete these phrases about blame?*

*Whenever I slip into blaming others I feel____*
*Seeing myself as a victim limits my ability to____*
*When I take responsibility*
*for my feelings, thoughts and actions I____*

# *Blessings*

Every moment we spend counting our blessings adds to the fullness and the richness of our lives.

Blessings are rarely something we earn. Usually they come to us as unexpected gifts. Our task, of course is to recognize them, especially when they feel negative at first.

Recognizing our blessings is rather like searching for stars on a dark, cloudy night. The more we accustom our eyes to looking for them, the more of them we are likely to see.

. ._._. . ._._. . ._._. . ._._. . ._._.

*How would you complete these phrases about blessings?*

*I feel especially grateful for___*
*A blessing I hadn't recognized until now is___*
*I could teach myself to see more blessings by___*

# Boundaries

All too often, we contribute to our own unhappiness by neglecting to set good limits for the way we allow others to treat us.

Creating a boundary is somewhat like wrapping ourselves with an invisible, thick rubber band. This imaginary outer limit keeps us from merging ourselves into other people's lives and also prevents them from merging into ours.

"It's not OK." These three simple words can help us to set limits without resorting to blame or guilt

*How would you complete these phrases about boundaries?*

*A time I didn't set good boundaries was___*
*A place in my life I could set better boundaries is___*
*Something that isn't OK for me to do*
*or for me to allow someone else to do to me is___*

# *Busyness*

When we schedule life too tightly, we leave no room for magic.

If we could remind ourselves that nothing beautiful or good is ever created all at once, we might be gentler with ourselves.  Maybe then we'd be less likely to run past the wonder of life in our frantic attempt to catch up with it.

Since it's easy to see that being superwoman is self-defeating, self-abusive and foolish, it's hard to understand our frequent willingness to try out for the part.

*How would you complete these phrases about busyness?*

*I know I'm too busy when____*
*One thing I could decide not to do today is____*
*I don't need to prove myself by__*

## *Personal Notes*

Balance_____

_____

_____

Being Enough_____

_____

_____

Being Loved_____

_____

_____

Beliefs_____

_____

_____

Blame_____

_____

_____

Blessings_____

_____

_____

Boundaries_____

_____

_____

Busyness_____

_____

_____

*Caring For Others,*
*Celebrating Our Uniqueness,*
*Change, Choice, Clarity,*
*Communication, Compassion,*
*Compromise, Connection, Contribution,*
*Control, Courage, Creativity*

# Caring For Others

Compassionate caring for others requires that we set our own judgments aside.

Just as we disempower others by assuming we know what they need, we empower them when we ask respectful questions about how we might participate in their greater happiness.

Since our attitudes, beliefs and actions affect the lives of those around us, one of the best ways to care for others is to make more positive and life-affirming choices for ourselves.

*How would you complete these phrases about caring for others?*

*A judgment I need to set aside is___*
*Someone I may have*
*disempowered by my assumptions is___*
*I could care for myself with more compassion by___*

## *Celebrating Our Uniqueness*

Celebrating our uniqueness frees us to do our own self-liking.  It helps us work toward building more fulfilling relationships with others because the fulfilling relationship we have with ourselves lets us know such things are possible.

Our uniqueness, and the courage it sometimes takes to express it, is one of the most precious gifts we have to give.

As we begin to acknowledge and celebrate our uniqueness, it's actually a relief to realize we're not everyone's cup of tea.

⋅⋏⋅ ⋅⋏⋅ ⋅⋏⋅ ⋅⋏⋅ ⋅⋏⋅

*How would you complete these phrases about celebrating your uniqueness?*

*I could create a better relationship with myself by___*
*Some of the ways I am unique are___*
*I could celebrate my own uniqueness by___*

## *Change*

The more we view change as something to
resist, the less we see and celebrate the treasures
that it holds.

Very little in our lives is likely to change until
we look for the changes we can make in ourselves.

Sometimes we need to empty our glasses in
order to refill them with something fresh and new.

*How would you complete these phrases about change?*

*A change in my life
that brought me great happiness was___
A change I'd like to make in myself is___
A change I'd like to make in my life is___*

# *Choice*

We are all partners in the dance of relationship. We are responsible for the steps we choose for ourselves and for the steps we leave to others. None of us are puppets. No one pulls our strings unless we give them permission. We are the ones who ultimately choose the way we do life's dance.

Choice comes in the form of thoughts as well as actions. Every time we choose a positive, life-affirming thought, we grow in our ability to live a happier, more rewarding life.

*How would you complete these phrases about choice?*

*Some of the good choices I've made for myself are____*
*Some of the positive, life-affirming thoughts*
*I have today are____*

# *Clarity*

The clearer we are about what we value, the easier it becomes to make the kinds of choices that can lead us to a fuller, richer life.

When we are absolutely clear about what we want, as well as our willingness to work for it, it's amazing how often it comes to us…in its own good time, of course.

·⌒·⌒·⌒·⌒·⌒·

*How would you complete these phrases about choices?*

*I'm absolutely clear that I value____*
*I'm absolutely clear that I am willing to work for____*

# Communication

"Should" and "ought" are guilt-provoking, disempowering words. They cause us to feel disappointed by the things we think and do. When we replace them with phrases such as "I choose, I need or I want to", we empower ourselves and add richness to our lives.

The word "but" almost always introduces a judgmental or negative thought. Replacing it with the word "and" helps us to make simple statements without slipping into negativity.

*How would you complete these phrases about communication?*

*One place in my life*
*that I could let go of the word "should" is____*
*Changing "but" to "and" in my conversations could____*

# *Compassion*

Compassion requires that we go beyond our need to forgive or understand. Compassion requires that we remember that all of us are fragile human beings, none of whom has been given an instruction manual for living a perfect life.

Compassion is a vital ingredient in a fuller and more meaningful life.

Living life with greater compassion toward ourselves helps us to live with greater compassion toward others.

*How would you change these phrases about compassion?*

*I need to have more compassion for___*
*A place in my life where I am already compassionate is___*
*I could show greater compassion for myself by___*

# *Compromise*

Compromise is usually about two people, each giving up something that is important to them.

Our task is to approach disagreements with a sense of creative co-authorship. We need to look beyond the limits of compromise in order to discover other possibilities.

⋅⌣⋅⌣⋅⌣⋅⌣⋅⌣⋅

*How would you complete these phrases about compromise?*

*I could participate in finding better solutions by___*
*Looking for other possibilities helps me to___*

# Connection

Each of us is like a link in a chain, complete by ourselves, yet seeking to become a part of something more than we can be alone.

Sometimes it's as though we see ourselves more clearly when we reach out to someone else, then recognize a part of who we are within them.

Life, like a necklace, is not just a random assortment of beads. Everything that gives it meaning and beauty is somehow connected. Our world is filled with people who are stringing their individual necklaces. While the beads they use may be different, it is this universal process that connects us all.

*How would you complete these phrases about connection?*

*Someone I would like to feel more connected to is___*
*Someone in whom I see myself is___*
*I feel more connected to others when___*

# Contribution

By creating peace within ourselves we participate in the creation of a more peaceful world.

Each of us makes a difference. What we do and how we live matters. Through our words and actions we can help others to weave a tangible cloth from the individual threads of their dreams. This is not about personal greatness. It is about the power in each of us to grow and change in such a way as to honor, nurture and respect both life and one another's dreams for it.

*How would you complete these phrases about contribution?*

*I could create a more peaceful life for myself by____*
*I could make more of a difference by____*

## *Control*

When we give up our need to control an ever widening spectrum of life, we usually feel more peaceful and self-contained.

What's so great about being in control when we have no real idea where this vehicle we call life is taking us?

It's particularly difficult to enjoy our lives when we are too busy whipping them into shape.

*How would you complete these about control?*

*When I try to control too much___*
*I feel more relaxed about my life when___*
*Just for today I could set aside my need to control___*

# Courage

Some of our greatest acts of courage seem somehow to be linked to love. Perhaps this means that the more we open ourselves to love, the more courageous we ultimately become.

Every time we act with authenticity or speak our truth with love and grace, we experience the kind of courage that is a building block for a fuller and more rewarding life.

As we begin to recognize our own small acts of courage we also begin to recognize the power of that courage.

*How would you complete these phrases about courage?*

*One of the ways love has given me courage is____*
*When I speak my truth with love and grace I feel____*
*One of the places in my life*
*where I recognize my own courage is__*

# *Creativity*

Creativity comes from the ability to see alternatives.

Creativity rarely comes when we demand its appearance. Creativity is born when we clear away the debris of old thinking so new thoughts and inspirations can get through.

Living more creatively helps us to live with fewer limitations.

*How would you complete these phrases about creativity?*

*A place in my life where I need to be*
*more aware of creative alternatives is___*
*I limit my creativity by___*
*One thing I could do to live more creatively is___*

# *C*

## *Personal Notes*

Caring For Others_____

_____

_____

Celebrating Our Uniqueness_____

_____

_____

Change_____

_____

_____

Choice_____

_____

_____

Clarity_____

_____

_____

Communication_____

_____

_____

Compassion_____

_____

_____

## *Personal Notes*

Compromise_____

_____

_____

Connection_____

_____

_____

Contribution_____

_____

_____

Control_____

_____

_____

Courage_____

_____

_____

Creativity_____

_____

_____

*Deadlines, Death, Decisions,*
*Declaration Of Our Potential For*
*Happiness, Denial, Depression,*
*Disappointment, Dishonesty,*
*Dreams,*

# Deadlines

Every time we create an arbitrary deadline, we interrupt the flow and joy of life. Choosing to rid ourselves of unnecessary deadlines helps us to become more available for life's gifts as they come to us.

All too often, the deadlines we create cause us to hurry through a task simply to complete it. They keep us from experiencing the joy that can often be found in the doing.

*How would you complete these phrases about deadlines?*

*An arbitrary deadline I could let go of is___*
*I could create more joy in the midst of my doing by___*

## *Death*

Perhaps we mourn not so much for the one
who has died as for ourselves and for the empty
space their leaving causes in our heart. Sometimes,
too, we grieve for the dreams we've had for the
relationship which never quite came true.

The miracle of loving touches this thing called
death. When we love someone, and they love
us, they seem to leave a part of themselves within
us when they die. Then, as time passes, we begin
to see and hear and feel with their eyes and ears
and hearts, as well as with our own. The deeper
our love, the more power this miracle has in our
lives. It is a constant and healing reminder that
we are never truly alone and there is only the
narrowest of streams that separates us from those
who have gone ahead. Love is the bridge that
crosses that stream.

*How would you complete these phrases about death?*

*Sometimes I grieve for____*
*Someone who has left a part of themselves within me is____*

# Decisions

What if we could change our lives by temporarily postponing our decisions and allowing ourselves more time to look for alternatives?

Many of the most important changes we make in life begin with our decision to make a change.

We must possess not only the courage to make decisions, but the wisdom and willingness to grow and learn from them, regardless of whether we're right or wrong.

*How would you complete these phrases about decisions?*

*A decision I could postpone making is___*
*A change I could decide to make is___*
*A decision I've learned from is___*

# *Declaration Of*
# *Our Potential For Happiness*

Survival is not enough for any of us. Struggle
is not our destiny. To learn merely from suffering
is not our life's work. We were created to learn
from all experiences. We were created to learn
from what is joyful and beautiful as well as
from what is painful and sad. Consciously
acknowledging our moments of contentment
helps us to see them as something we can
re-create. Participating in this sort of creation
takes us to a place in life that far exceeds
mere survival.

*How would you complete this phrase about declaring your
potential for happiness?*

*I participate in creating my own happiness by____*

# Denial

Where do our feelings go if we deny or dismiss them? Perhaps they simply hide under some black, slippery rock and lay waiting for us there.

The more skillful we are at denying our feelings, the more we need to work on staying truthful with ourselves.

*How would you complete these phrases about denial?*

*When I deny my feelings___*
*I could stay more truthful to myself by___*

# *Depression*

Depression robs our life of color. It keeps us from noticing our blessings, from making decisions and from seeing possibilities. Depression is a sad but sometimes necessary reminder that we need to be kinder to ourselves.

Since feelings of depression tend to feed upon themselves, sometimes we need to alter our emotional diet with thoughts of our reasons to feel grateful.

One of the ways to move beyond the inertia of depression is to ask ourselves what small action we could take, then encourage ourselves to take it.

*How would you complete these phrases about depression?*

*I could be kinder to myself by____*
*Some of my reasons for feeling grateful are____*
*One small action I could take right now is____*

# *Disappointment*

We have the power to change the course of our days by changing how long we hold on to our disappointments.

Even though we might feel disappointed if we don't reach our dreams, we're likely to feel more disappointed if we don't try to reach them.

Focusing too long on our disappointments can cause them to expand until they form an enormous emotional oil slick, polluting both our thoughts and our lives.

*How would you complete these phrases about disappointment?*

*Once I've acknowledged my disappointment it helps to ___*
*A dream I am determined to reach for is___*
*One disappointment I could let go of is___*

# *Dishonesty*

Whenever we need to reassure ourselves that we're managing just fine, it's possible that we're not being fully honest with ourselves.

How often in life do we contribute to our own unhappiness by lying to ourselves?

If we stay silent about things that truly need to be said, our silence creates a wordless form of dishonesty.

*How would you complete these phrases about dishonesty?*

*I need to be more honest with myself about___*
*Being more truthful with myself helps me to___*
*I need to be more honest with others about___*

# Dreams

Whenever we are given dreams, we are also given the ability to make some part of those dreams come true…especially if we're willing to work for them.

Working to make our dreams come true is one of the most positive and empowering forms of self-caring.

While the attainment of our dreams may lie in the future, the path to those dreams begins at our feet. Looking for the parts of our dreams that already exist in our lives helps us to build on them.

*How would you complete these phrases about dreams?*

*A dream I am willing to work toward is___*
*An immediate small step I could take toward my dream is___*
*The parts of my dream that are already in my life are__*

# *D*

## *Personal Notes*

Deadlines_____

_____

_____

Death_____

_____

_____

Decisions_____

_____

_____

Declaration Of Our Potential For Happiness_____

_____

_____

Denial_____

_____

_____

Depression_____

_____

_____

Disappointment_____

_____

_____

## *Personal Notes*

Dishonesty_____

_____

_____

Dreams_____

_____

_____

*Earning Love, Effort and*
*Effortlessness, Empty Spaces,*
*Expectation*

## *Earning Love*

The kind of love we are able to earn seldom truly nurtures us.

When we're trying to earn love, our focus is actually on ourselves and on what we want from someone else. Maybe that's why working to earn love feels so empty and unsatisfying so much of the time.

If we're content to be loved for only the parts of ourselves we are willing to let others see, we'll need to spend the rest of our lives pretending the other parts of us don't exist. Ultimately this kind of deception creates an inwardly lonely way to live.

*How would you complete these phrases about earning love?*

> *The kind of love that truly nurtures me is___*
> *When I'm not so focused on being loved___*
> *A part of myself I hide in order to be loved is___*

## Effort and Effortlessness

The greatest effort in life often comes from
trying to shape our experiences to fit our
expectations.  How much more satisfying it is
to simply acknowledge an experience, then work
toward using it for our continuing growth.

What if our belief in the power of continual
effort keeps us from letting go and enjoying
the experience of effortlessness?

The clearer we are about what is truly important,
the less effort we expend on what is not.

*How would you complete these phrases about effort and
effortlessness?*

*An experience I need to simply acknowledge is____*
*Something I could change that would*
*make one part of my life more effortless is____*
*A part of life that is truly important to me is____*

## *Empty Spaces*

We usually feel the greatest emptiness within us when we've allowed the outer part of our lives to become too full.

If some of the pieces seem to be temporarily missing from our life's puzzle, perhaps the space that's left empty provides a place for discovery and growth.

Silence is that blessed empty space that often feeds and fills us.

*How would you complete these phrases about empty spaces?*

*I could create a more healing space in my life by____*
*An empty space in my life that has helped me to grow is____*
*Whenever I'm in a silent space I notice____*

## *Expectation*

Expectation is the enemy of flow, the enemy of love, the enemy of appreciation. Expectation is the enemy of limitlessness, the enemy of creativity and the enemy of living a happier, more possibility filled life.

While expectations limit our sense of possibility, a sense of wonder and curiosity expands it. Whenever we let go of our expectations, we open the door to possibilities we may not have noticed before.

When we're feeling badly because we don't measure up to someone else's expectations, we need to look more closely at the yardstick they are using.

*How would you complete these phrases about expectation?*

*An expectation that diminished my happiness was___*
*An expectation I could let go of is___*
*Some of my unrealistic expectations are___*

## *Personal Notes*

Earning Love_____

_____

_____

Effort and Effortlessness_____

_____

_____

Empty Spaces_____

_____

_____

Expectations_____

_____

_____

*Failure, Fairness, Faith, Fear,*
*Fixing, Focus, Forgiveness,*
*Freedom From Within, Frenzy,*
*Fun, Future*

## *Failure*

When we're focused on how afraid we are at the thought of failing, it's much harder to take the small, simple steps that could lead us to richer fuller lives.

When we look more closely at what seems to be a failure, we often discover the roots of our eventual success.

Perhaps the only true failure in life is the failure to keep on learning and growing.

*How would you complete these phrases about failure?*

*One small step I could take toward a richer, fuller life is___*
*A failure I have learned from is___*
*Something I need to learn more about is___*

## *Fairness*

Perhaps we need to give up the belief that if we're fair with someone, they'll be fair with us in return. It isn't necessarily true. Fairness is simply a part of who we are. We can't offer it to someone else with the absolute assurance of getting it back.

*How would you complete this phrase about fairness?*

*Whenever I attach an expectation to my sense of fairness*
*I notice____*

# *Faith*

Even though we are often confronted by the angry, hostile parts of life, kindness and humanity are still the largest, truest reality. Every moment we spend noticing life's basic goodness is a moment spent feeling more contented and fulfilled.

Faith comes in many forms; faith in a creator, faith in a plan we don't always understand, faith in ourselves and others or simply faith in life itself. Whatever our personal faiths, the more we draw them to us and make them an ongoing part of our lives, the more inwardly peaceful we become.

*How would you complete these phrases about faith?*

*Some of the goodness in life I have noticed is___*
*I could make my faith*
*more of an ongoing part of my life by___*

# *Fear*

The less we look for possibility, the more fearful we are likely to feel. Our unwillingness to seek options locks our fear inside us. A sense of possibility gives us a key to unlock that door.

Since most of the fear we feel lies in the future, one of the best antidotes for fearfulness is to focus on the positive actions and attitudes that can help us in the present. The fears we feel for tomorrow rarely keep us safe today.

What if our fearfulness for others diminishes their courage for themselves?

*How would you complete these phrases about fear?*

*I am more aware of possibilities when____*
*A positive attitude I could carry with me in the present is____*
*I could help others to feel more courageous by____*

# *Fixing*

It's especially tempting to try to fix some people.
Usually they're the ones who haven't yet learned
to get out from under the toilet of heaven when
it flushes.

Thinking we can fix someone else is a colossal
form of arrogance. How can we possibly know
what others may need in their journey through
life when we can't fully know that for ourselves?

When we assume that someone needs fixing, we
diminish our ability to believe in and encourage
them. To love them enough to stand beside them,
is a much more empowering and lasting kind
of love.

*How would you complete these phrases about fixing?*

*Someone I've been trying too hard to fix is____*
*When I make assumptions about others I notice____*
*I could become more empowering by____*

## *Focus*

One of the miracles of the way we were created
is that we can only focus on one thing at a time.
This means every moment we spend seeing the
blessings in our lives is a moment we're not using
to focus on our disappointments.

If we wish to live happier, more empowering lives,
we need to be continually aware of our focus.

As long as we use our energy to focus on what
is wrong with life, we can't utilize that same
energy to explore our choices.

*How would you complete these phrases about focus?*

*Some of the many blessings in my life are____*
*When I'm focusing on what I am grateful for I feel____*
*I could teach myself to*
*become more aware of my choices by____*

## *Forgiveness*

The more we gather information, the more understanding we become. The more understanding we become, the less we need to judge. The less we need to judge, the more we see with compassionate eyes. The more we see with compassionate eyes, the clearer it becomes how very little in life really needs our forgiveness.

Neither judgment nor forgiveness is truly necessary when we view our world with compassionate eyes.

Since we simply don't have enough information about anyone else's life, the only person we can truly judge, then choose to forgive, is ourselves.

* ⌃ · ⌃ · ⌃ · ⌃ · ⌃ ·

*How would you complete these phrases about forgiveness?*

*Someone I could see with more compassion is___*
*When I look at others with compassionate eyes___*
*I could be less judgmental toward myself about___*

## *Freedom From Within*

Genuine inner freedom begins with the decision to think and act from the authentic core of who we truly are. We need to be continually vigilant in protecting this freedom, since we are the ones who are most likely to steal it from ourselves.

⋅᠁⋅⋅᠁⋅⋅᠁⋅⋅᠁⋅⋅᠁⋅

*How would you complete this phrase about freedom from within?*

*When I act from the authentic core of who I am____*

# *Frenzy*

Even though most of us can run faster in our minds than anyone we know, the more frenzied we become, the less we are likely to feel fulfilled and contented in our lives.

Feeling frenzied gets in the way of communication. It gets in the way of productivity. It gets in the way of loving and of living a happy and contented life.

The clearer we are about those things that are truly important in our lives, the easier it becomes to set aside our frenzy and to direct our energy toward the tasks that enhance our sense of inner peace.

*How would you complete these phrases about frenzy?*

*A part of my frenzy I could choose to set aside is____*
*When I am feeling frenzied I also notice that I'm feeling____*
*The deepest and most truly important parts of my life are____*

## *Fun*

While we may plan for fun in the future, we can only experience it in the present. Whenever we notice we aren't having much fun, chances are we're focusing too much on the future.

Life is very precious and the capacity for experiencing fun lives within our minds. If something isn't fun or if we can't create an element of fun around it, perhaps we might consider not doing it.

*How would you complete these phrases about fun?*

*I could include more fun in my life by___*
*Something around which I could create*
*more of a sense of fun is___*

# Future

Whenever we're too focused on the future we diminish our ability to live, to learn from and to fully appreciate what our lives hold in the present.

Life is always about balance.  If we don't create a plan for the future, we risk living in confusion and endless disarray.  If, however, we don't live more fully in the present, we risk not truly living at all.

We participate in the creation of our future through the attitudes and actions that form our present lives.

*How would you complete these phrases about the future?*

*When I'm more focused on the present I notice that___*
*I can bring my thoughts back to the present by___*
*Some of my actions and attitudes that affect my future are___*

## *Personal Notes*

Failure_____

_____

_____

Fairness_____

_____

_____

Faith_____

_____

_____

Fear_____

_____

_____

Fixing_____

_____

_____

Focus_____

_____

_____

# *Personal Notes*

Forgiveness_____

_____

_____

Freedom From Within_____

_____

_____

Frenzy_____

_____

_____

Fun_____

_____

_____

Future_____

_____

_____

*Gentleness, Getting Through,*
*Giving, Goals, God's Plan,*
*Gratitude, Guilt*

# *Gentleness*

There is an unexpected, yet undeniable power in gentleness. When we stand for our beliefs with quiet harmlessness, we diminish the defensiveness of others. Authentic gentleness builds trust and creates a safe haven for self exploration and healing.

There is a vast difference between gentleness and weakness. While weakness often grows from unconscious habit, the power of true gentleness is built on conscious choice.

*How would you complete these phrases about gentleness?*

*Someone who has touched me with their gentleness is___*
*I could become more powerfully gentle by___*

# Getting Through

It's much more empowering to focus on the steps we are taking in the present than it is to focus on the final completion of a task.

When we work at a task just so we can get through it, our focus is usually on the future and on the pleasure we'll feel once it's completed. When we're mindful of the moments contained within that task, we have the opportunity to make more of them pleasurable.

Getting through something just so we can have it behind us diminishes the sense of joy and fulfillment that is possible in our lives.

*How would you complete these phrases about getting through?*

*Staying in the present helps me to____*
*A part of a task I can make more pleasurable is____*
*Something in one of my tasks that I appreciate is____*

# Giving

Whenever we give simply to stay even, our sense of anxious obligation diminishes the quality of our gift.

When we give in order to receive something in return, we rarely receive as much as we give. When we give without the thought of receiving, we are usually given much more.

What if our inappropriate over-giving causes others to feel that their gifts aren't as worthy or important in comparison?

*How would you complete these phrases about giving?*

*Sometimes I feel anxiously obligated toward___*
*When my desire to give truly comes from my heart___*
*Someone to whom I sometimes over-give is___*

# Goals

If we don't have goals, we're much less likely to take risks. If we don't take risks, we're much less likely to learn and grow.

Perhaps the difference between someone who feels successful and someone who does not, lies in the conscious decision to walk toward those things in life that contribute to their personal definition of success.

To participate in life rather than to be its victim is an important goal. Choosing to strive for that goal is one of life's most empowering choices.

*How would you complete these phrases about goals?*

*A risk I am glad to have taken is___*
*My definition of success is___*
*Something I am doing now that helps me feel successful is___*

## God's Plan

Since we don't have a broad enough vantage point
from which to view the intricate weaving of our
Creator's plan, sometimes it feels as though we live
on the backside of a tapestry where all we see are the
loose threads poking out.

Sometimes when we feel anxious, it helps to look
back over our lives in order to notice how much of
what we've needed has actually been given to us.

What if there is no such thing as coincidence?

*How would you complete these phrases about God's plan?*

*I need to have more faith about___*
*Some of my needs that have already been filled are___*
*Something in my life*
*that seems to be part of a greater plan is___*

## Gratitude

Gratitude is the golden key that unlocks the door to contentment and joy.

Gratitude helps us to notice what we already have. When we're lost on the path of disappointment or fear, gratitude is the signpost that helps us find our way back to a happier, more balanced life.

Choosing to live with a sense of gratitude changes and enriches every moment of our lives.

*How would you complete these phrases about gratitude?*

*Some of the things for which I feel grateful are____*
*I could teach myself to become more aware of*
*my reasons for gratitude by____*
*When I feel grateful I notice that I also feel____*

# Guilt

Guilt is something we give ourselves when we feel we haven't lived up to either our own or to someone else's expectations. Sometimes, though, we need to ask ourselves if those expectations are reasonable.

While we are continually responsible for treating others with compassion, we are not continually responsible for their happiness. Until we fully understand the difference, we'll probably always feel a little guilty.

When we find ourselves thinking that we "should" do something, we risk getting caught in a net of self-judgment and guilt. When we tell ourselves that we "need or want" to do the very same thing, we become empowered by our sense of responsibility and choice.

*How would you complete these phrases about guilt?*

*One of my unreasonable expectations is___*
*Something for which I am not responsible is___*
*Whenever I say "I should" I notice that___*

# *G*

## *Personal Notes*

Gentleness_____

_____

_____

Getting Through_____

_____

_____

Giving_____

_____

_____

Goals_____

_____

_____

God's Plan_____

_____

_____

Gratitude_____

_____

_____

Guilt_____

_____

_____

*Happiness, Helplessness,*
*Holding On, Honesty, Hope,*
*Humanity, Humility, Humor*

# Happiness

Happiness is a fresh and ever-flowing stream
and each of us has the power to choose the size
of the dipper we use to drink from it.

When we give someone else the power to make
us happy, we also give them the power to make
us unhappy. In the end, we are the only ones
who have the power to create ongoing happiness
for ourselves.

When we are feeling inwardly happy, it's a
disservice to others to pretend that we're not.
Honoring our own happiness as we treat those
who are less happy with compassion, creates
the sort of atmosphere in which greater
happiness seems possible.

*How would you complete these phrases about happiness?*

*I could increase the happiness I feel in life by___*
*I need to share my happiness more honestly with___*

# Helplessness

Whenever we see ourselves as weak or helpless, we participate in keeping ourselves in that place.

Helplessness is a disempowering disease that prevents us from assuming reasonable responsibility for our lives. Fortunately the phrase, "I can do it over time," is usually a fairly painless cure.

While seeming weak and helpless keeps us from accepting full responsibility for our lives, doing the best we can each day empowers and fulfills us.

⋅⌒⋅⋅⌒⋅⋅⌒⋅⋅⌒⋅⋅⌒⋅

*How would you complete these phrases about helplessness?*

*Something strong and capable I notice about myself is____*
*Something I could accomplish over time is____*
*I need to accept more responsibility for____*

## *Holding On*

Holding on to negative feelings is a little like holding onto the blade of a knife. The person it usually hurts most is the person doing the holding.

Sometimes we hold onto limiting beliefs simply because we're unwilling to commit to the temporary discomfort of making a place in our minds for something new.

When we hold onto those we love by intertwining our lives too tightly with theirs, we reduce the possibility that either of us will experience and celebrate our full uniqueness and individuality.

*How would you complete these phrases about holding on?*

*A negative feeling I no longer need to hold onto is___*
*One of my beliefs that limits my ability to be fully happy is___*
*Someone I need to hold onto less tightly is___*

## *Honesty*

Honesty is an essential part of honor. If we
do not value the truth and speak it with
compassion and grace, we tarnish and diminish
the quality of our lives.

Although honesty will ultimately set us free,
first we may need to clear up the dishonesty
that has been part of our life in the past.

The most empowering form of honesty is
being honest with ourselves.

*How would you complete these phrases about honesty?*

*Someone to whom I need to be more truthful is____*
*Something I need to be more honest about is____*
*The price I pay for being dishonest with myself is____*

# *Hope*

There is nothing quite so strong or quite as
fragile as our ability to hope.

Healthy hoping helps us hold a place in our
hearts for improbable possibilities. Unhealthy
hoping keeps us stuck in limiting experiences.

Hope is a vital part of a positive, potential-filled
life. We need, however, to attach action to our
hopes in order to be empowered by them.

*How would you complete these phrases about hopefulness?*

*I feel hopeful about____*
*It is unhealthy for me to continue hoping that____*
*An empowering action I could take right now is____*

# *Humanity*

Most of us fall short of our vision of perfection. While we strive to be strong, sometimes instead we feel fragile or afraid. While we strive to behave lovingly, all too often our resentments create a barrier to that love. While we strive to heal, there are times we inadvertently wound. It is the space between who we are and who we long to be that gives us our humanity. It is this space that connects us with one another. It is this space that requires each of us to love and forgive ourselves as well as others, despite our inconsistency and our seeming flaws and failures.

⋅⋅⋅⋅⋅⋅⋅⋅⋅⋅⋅⋅

*How would you complete this phrase about humanity?*

*I see my own humanity reflected in____*

# *Humility*

There is something wrong with a definition of humility that keeps us from gratefully acknowledging the positive parts of who we are.

While pride and arrogance are is rooted in the belief that we are somehow the source of the goodness in our lives, humility is rooted in the sure knowledge that we are a channel through which life's goodness flows.

*How would you complete these phrases about humility?*

*Some of the positive parts of myself*
*that I gratefully acknowledge are____*
*Living with a greater sense of humility*
*could help me to____*

# *Humor*

Humor is the lubricant that oils the wheels of life. Unfortunately we often neglect to apply that precious friction reducer because we're moving just a little too fast.

Sometimes, sadly, we use humor to mask the pain or disappointment we are feeling in our hearts.

Imagine how much happier our lives might become if we looked for reasons to laugh at both ourselves and life more often.

*How would you complete these phrases about humor?*

*One of the ways I could add humor to my life is___*
*A time I used humor as a mask was___*
*A part of my life I could take less seriously is___*

## *Personal Notes*

Happiness_____

_____

_____

Helplessness_____

_____

_____

Holding On_____

_____

_____

Honesty_____

_____

_____

Hope_____

_____

_____

Humanity_____

_____

_____

Humility_____

_____

_____

Humor_____

_____

*Independence, Inner Child,*
*Inner Voice, Inspiration,*
*Integrity, Interdependence*

# *Independence*

The more we see and celebrate our own uniqueness, the less we are willing to be shaped by the world around us. The less we are willing to be shaped by the world around us, the more courageously independent we become.

When we are true to our values, our sense of independence becomes more effortless and natural.

*How would you complete this phrase about independence?*

*I feel courageously independent about___*
*One of my values*
*that can help me to become more independent is___*

# *Inner Child*

If our inner child is filled with wonder,
spontaneity, love and acceptance, why do we
assign such value to behaving like an adult?

Every time we look at life with wonder or with
a sense of curiosity, we honor the child within
us and expand our sense of possibility.

*How would you complete these phrases about your inner child?*

*I could act from the inner child part of myself
more often by___*
*The last time I looked at life with a sense of wonder was___*

# *Inner Voice*

Sometimes we're so busy looking for guidance from the outside world we forget to listen for the quiet voice within us. It is this wise and gentle voice that connects us to our values and helps us to become clearer and more compassionate.

We need to listen to our inner voices in order to give ourselves the gifts of peacefulness and balance. Expecting others to give us these gifts almost always leads to feelings of disappointment, dependence and disempowerment.

*How would you complete these phrases about your inner voice?*

*Listening to my inner voice has helped me to____*
*I hear my inner voice more clearly when____*

# Inspiration

The thoughts that come to us as gifts from our unconscious minds form a bridge between an ordinary life and that place beyond it we call inspiration. The more we notice and honor those thoughts as they come to us, the more centered and creative our lives are likely to become.

In order to live in the light of this thing we call inspiration, we need to make a space in our thinking for something that lies beyond logic, reason and practicality.

The more we look for those things in life that light our inner fire, the more connected we become to our sense of inspiration.

*How would you complete these phrases about inspiration?*

*A thought that once came to me as a gift was____*
*I could leave more space for inspiration by____*
*Something that lights my inner fire is____*

# *Integrity*

To live with greater integrity we need to make fewer promises, then to do everything in our power to keep the ones we've made.

.˄. .˄. .˄. .˄. .˄.

*How would you complete this phrase about integrity?*

*A promise I've already made that I need to keep is____*

# *Interdependence*

There is great power in interdependence. It is the interdependence of independent columns that supports the weight of a roof. It is the interdependence of sun and rain that give us both food and flowers. It is the interdependence of unique and independent people that brings the greatest sense of fulfillment and possibility to the world in which we live.

*How would you complete this phrase about interdependence?*

*Someone with whom I have a healthy sense of interdependence is____*

# *Personal Notes*

Independence_____

_____

_____

Inner Child_____

_____

_____

Inner Voice_____

_____

_____

Inspiration_____

_____

_____

Integrity_____

_____

_____

Interdependence_____

_____

_____

*Journal-Keeping, The Journey,*
*Joy, Judgment*

# Journal-Keeping

Keeping a journal is like using a broom. It helps us to sweep out the dust and debris that is stuck in the corners of our minds.

Because writing is slower than thinking, keeping a journal helps us take more time with our thoughts. It helps us become more compassionate and peaceful because it gives us a tool for exploring and healing our own lives.

*How would you complete these phrases about journal keeping?*

*The first thing I'd like to write about in a journal is___*
*Something I could set aside*
*so I could begin keeping a journal today is___*

# The Journey

When we're feeling disappointed with ourselves for needing to relearn the lessons of life, it's helpful to remember that we are on a spiral journey. Each time we come upon a lesson we thought we'd already learned, we have the opportunity to learn more from it, because we v iew it from a slightly different vantage point.

A journey is composed of countless steps, each of which is important. Neglecting to honor our steps as we take them creates the kind of discouragement that can cause us to stop too soon. We need to continually remind ourselves that small steps taken every day can create great changes over time.

*How would you complete these phrases about your journey?*

*Something I must still need to learn*
*that keeps appearing in my life is____*
*A small step that could help me make a necessary change is____*

## *Joy*

Joy is a feeling we were created to experience.
Joy is a part of life that belongs to us more fully
when we are more aware of its ongoing presence.
Joy is a necessary and vital part of a powerful,
meaningful life.

In order to learn from joy, we need to honor it
as it comes to us. We also need to teach ourselves
to notice the many places it already exists in
our life.

While it may be true that the pain that doesn't
kill makes us stronger, imagine how much
happier our lives might be if we also taught
ourselves to learn from what is joyful.

*How would you complete these phrases about joy?*

*I feel the most joyful when I am____*
*A place in my life that already feels joyful is____*
*Something I've learned from a joyful experience is____*

# Judgment

Every time we pre-judge a situation or person
based on past experience we limit our ability
to see what is truly there.

If we want to be a part of relationships that
contain humor, grace and acceptance, judging
others for not being more like us isn't very helpful.

Every time we talk about people behind their
backs, or stretch the truth, or base our decisions
on judgment rather than understanding, we
contribute to the poison that pollutes our universe.
Every time we act with compassion, honesty
and integrity we participate in the powerful
possibility that our planet may one day be healed.
This makes our lives and the spirit with which
we live them of the utmost importance and
consequence.

*How would you complete these phrases about judgment?*
*Someone I once pre-judged is___*
*I need to be less judgmental toward___*

## *Personal Notes*

Journal-Keeping_____

_____

_____

The Journey_____

_____

_____

Joy_____

_____

_____

Judgment_____

_____

_____

*Kindness, Knowledge*

# Kindness

Sometimes our expectations keep us from
noticing the simple acts of kindness we are
already receiving in our lives.

One of the kindest things we do for others
is to acknowledge the kindness they show
toward us.

Imagine what our lives might be like if we
practiced just one more act of kindness
each day.

⁘ ⸱ ⸱⸱⸱ ⸱⸱⸱ ⸱⸱⸱ ⸱⸱ ⁘

*How would you complete these phrases about kindness?*

*A time when my expectations kept me*
*from noticing a simple act of kindness was___*
*Someone whose kindness I need to acknowledge is___*
*One kind thing I could do today is___*

# Knowledge

Knowledge comes from observation and experience just as surely as it comes from books.

Knowledge, like love, has a way of multiplying when we share it appropriately.

The more we strive to gather knowledge, the more self confident we become. The more self confident we become the more we are able to participate in relationships that are mutually respectful.

*How would you complete these phrases about knowledge?*

*Something I've observed today is____*
*Someone from whom I often learn is____*
*Something I feel confident about is____*

## *Personal Notes*

Kindness_____

_____

_____

Knowledge_____

_____

_____

*Lack, Learning, Letting Go,*
*Limitations, Limitlessness,*
*Listening, Living, Loose Ends,*
*Loneliness, Love*

## Lack

How often, when something good comes to us, do we keep ourselves from truly savoring it by worrying about how long it will last?

Focusing on what we are lacking in life rarely makes us happy. Focusing instead on the actions we might take to fill our lives more fully empowers us and expands our sense of abundance.

*How would you complete these phrases about lack?*

*I could savor the goodness in my life more fully by___*
*When I focus on those things*
*that are abundant in my life, I notice that___*

# *Learning*

To be continually learning is to be continually alive.

Acknowledging how little we know helps us to live our lives with a perpetual sense of wonder and curiosity.

The more fun it is to learn, the more we feel invited in by the process. While we often apply this principle to children, sometimes, as adults, we forget to apply it for ourselves.

*How would you complete these phrases about learning?*

*Something new I've learned today is____*
*I'm often amazed by____*
*I could add more fun to what I am presently learning by____*

# Letting Go

What if people are like flowers? What if our hovering over them in order to protect them, actually robs them of the sunshine and raindrops they may need for their optimal growth?

Letting go of those we love does not mean abandoning them. Letting go simply means releasing them from the fears and expectations we may have for them. It means walking beside them on their chosen paths, rather than expecting them to follow the paths we may have wanted them to take.

*How would you complete these phrases about letting go?*

*Someone over whom I may be hovering is____*
*An expectation I need to let go of is____*

# Limitations

Perhaps the secret of happiness lies in seeing the wonder of life, even within the boundaries of our limitations.

Perhaps we limit what we are able to receive from life because we're so focused on wanting something else that we don't notice what we're actually receiving.

The most limiting phrase in any language is, "I can't."

*How would you complete these phrases about limitations?*

*When I look for possibilities instead of problems___*
*Something I've received that I have not yet acknowledged is___*
*Something I need to stop thinking I can't do is___*

# Limitlessness

The most limitless phrase in any language is,
"I think I can do a part of that now."

What we focus on in life is truly what we see.
While focusing on our limitations can make
us feel small and powerless, focusing instead
on a search for what is possible enriches and
enlivens every facet of our lives.

*How would you complete these phrases about limitlessness?*

*Something I can do a part of now is____*
*A place in my life where I could begin a search for*
*more possibility is____*

# Listening

What we say to others is usually far less important than the way we listen to them. Listening without searching for words to respond, keeps our hearts open to what is truly being said.

Since we can't really listen when we are feeling defensive, the less we take things personally the more we are able to truly hear.

While we may not always agree with those we love, listening to them with respectfulness and compassion keeps conversation flowing. Listening creates a bridge toward greater understanding.

*How would you complete these phrases about listening?*

*Someone who needs me to listen more fully is___*
*Something I feel defensive about*
*that has diminished my ability to listen is___*
*When I listen with compassion I notice that___*

# Living

What do our calendars know about living
when they only know about scheduling?
When we schedule our days too tightly, we
become as lacking in aliveness as the calendars
on our walls.

Today, on this blank page of life, we have the
power to create new memories, to redirect our
focus and to make the kinds of choices that
make the word "living" a truly magnificent verb.

*How would you complete these phrases about living?*

*Something I don't really need to do today is___*
*I could make "living" a more meaningful verb by___*

# *Loose Ends*

Just like an untied shoelace, it's the little loose
ends of life that tend to trip us up.


Every time we leave a task without completing
it, we need to draw on our precious energy to
return to it again.


*How would you complete these phrases about loose ends?*

*My incomplete tasks contribute to my feelings of____
A task I need to complete today is____*

## *Loneliness*

Loneliness is having a gift to give and finding no one to receive it. Loneliness is fullness, waiting to be shared.

Since loneliness exists to some extent in all of us, perhaps it was created as a meeting place between our Creator and ourselves.

*How would you complete these phrases about loneliness?*

*Some of my gifts that I'd like to give to others are___*
*Something important I discovered when I was lonely was___*

# Love

Love is a gift that chooses us more easily when we are not trying to manipulate someone else's feelings by being something we are not. Love chooses us when we risk being our full selves, when we take off our protective layers, when we are authentic and when we are willing to not be loved in order to be true to who we are.

Love is not a promise of constant joy. Rather it is a promise of moving beyond and through and around our human limitations in order to help one another hold a basket for the miracles of life.

We get so funny about love, so sugar-sweet, so wrapped up in romance. At its deepest level, love is about people managing to support and celebrate each other in spite of their differences and in the midst of their individual growth.

*How would you complete this phrase about love?*
*Some of the people I truly love are___*

## *Personal Notes*

Lack_____

_____

_____

Learning_____

_____

_____

Letting Go_____

_____

_____

Limitations_____

_____

_____

Limitlessness_____

_____

_____

Listening_____

_____

_____

## *Personal Notes*

Living_____

_____

_____

Loose Ends_____

_____

_____

Loneliness_____

_____

_____

Love_____

_____

_____

*Making A Difference, Martyrdom,*
*Meaning Well, Memories,*
*Mission Impossible, Our Mission,*
*Mistakes, Moments, Money,*
*Mothers and Daughters*

## Making A Difference

We can't be of real service to others when we are feeling frenzied or overwhelmed. If we wish to make a lasting difference, we need to approach life with more centered and peaceful hearts. We can't help anyone else escape life's quicksand if we ourselves aren't standing on firm ground.

Imagine what a difference each of us might make if one of our daily goals was to leave both things and people just a little better than we found them?

*How would you complete these phrases about making a difference?*

*Some of the ways I already make a difference are___*
*Something I could leave better than I found it is___*

# Martyrdom

Believing we need to endure pain or hardship in order to truly care for those we love, diminishes the quality of our lives and falsely teaches others that martyrdom is synonymous with love.

The unhealthy hoping of martyrdom focuses on how others must change so that we can be happy. Focusing instead on how we ourselves can change, replaces that sense of martyrdom with self esteem and confidence.

·ᴧ· ·ᴧ· ·ᴧ· ·ᴧ· ·ᴧ·

*How would you complete these phrases about martyrdom?*

*I behave like a martyr when____*
*A change I could make in myself*
*that would empower me is____*

## Meaning Well

"She meant well" is probably not the inscription
most of us want on our tombstones.

Whenever we inflict our unsolicited opinions
on those we are hoping to help, we risk
diminishing their sense of confidence as well
as the quality of our relationship.

The more we are focused on living our own
lives with integrity and love, the less we are
tempted to begin any sentence with "You should".

*How would you complete these phrases about meaning well?*

*Since meaning well is not enough, I also need to___*
*Someone whose confidence I may have diminished is___*
*When I refrain from offering unsolicited advice*
*I notice that___*

# Memories

Since today's actions will become tomorrow's memories, we need to become more fully aware of the kinds of memories we truly wish to create.

Since our lives are built upon both positive and negative memories, focusing on those memories that have given us the greatest sense of happiness will help us to live more peaceful and powerful lives.

*How would you complete these phrases about memories?*

*A memory I could begin to create today is___*
*Some of my memories that have given me*
*the greatest sense of happiness are___*

## Mission Impossible

Since we're the only ones we have the real power to change, trying to change anyone else is truly an impossible mission.

⌣⌢⌣⌢⌣⌢⌣⌢⌣

*How would you complete this phrase about mission impossible?*

*Something I need to change about myself is___*

## *Our Mission*

By choosing happiness and contentment for ourselves we clear a path for others to make that choice as well.

*How would you complete this phrase about your mission?*

*I could create more happiness and contentment in my own life by___*

## *Mistakes*

Mistakes are a part of the learning process.  If we never risk, we rarely make mistakes.  Fearfully remembering past mistakes keeps us from taking reasonable risks and from living with hope and happiness in the present.

Mistakes are simply stepping stones toward potential success.  Each of the pots a potter discards improves his chances of making a better one.

*How would you complete these phrases about mistakes?*

*One of the successful risks I have taken is___*
*Some of my mistakes*
*that have helped me to live a richer life are___*

# *Moments*

Living with a sense of gratitude for each moment as it comes to us is the ultimate definition of self-caring.

We give away our power and our sense of possibility when we are not present in the moment.

They do count for something, all those little caring moments. They do add up. The big generous experiences may be important in our lives, but it is the accumulation of the little, almost forgotten, moments that shape us.

*How would you complete these phrases about moments?*

*In this present moment I feel grateful for____*
*When I am more present in the moment I notice that____*
*Something caring and generous of spirit*
*that I could do today is____*

# *Money*

Sometimes our relationship with money is rather like our relationship with the man who fixes our car. We like him, we need him and we appreciate him, but we're afraid of paying too much attention to him for fear of getting dirty.

Every time we say "It's only money" we speak disrespectfully about it. What if our disrespectful attitude toward money actually keeps us from having more of it in our lives?

* * *

*How would you complete these phrases about money?*

*Paying more attention to what I do with and what I believe about money would help me to___*
*I could treat money more respectfully by___*

# Mothers and Daughters

We're likely to be the most defensive about being like our mothers when we're focusing on their weaknesses or mistakes. When we acknowledge their strengths and successes, we become more able to celebrate those positive parts of who they are that also belong to us.

How long will daughters use their mothers as measuring sticks for how well they themselves are doing? How many of us choose to see our mothers as flawed, rather than simply as different, than we may have wanted them to be? What might happen if we chose to see them with greater compassion, gently accepting their example as a part of the life's lesson we may have been placed on earth to learn?

*How would you complete these phrases about mothers and daughters?*

*The parts of my mother I appreciate in myself are____*
*Seeing my mother with greater compassion helps me to____*

## *Personal notes*

Making A Difference_____

_____

_____

Martyrdom_____

_____

_____

Meaning Well_____

_____

_____

Memories_____

_____

_____

Mission Impossible_____

_____

_____

Our Mission_____

_____

_____

## *Personal notes*

Mistakes_____

_____

_____

Moments_____

_____

_____

Money_____

_____

_____

Mothers and Daughters_____

_____

_____

*Needing, Neediness, Needs,*
*Negativity, Niceness,*
*Not About Us, Noticing, Now*

# *Needing*

Part of the myth of loving is that if someone
cares enough about us they will fill our needs
without being asked.  The danger in believing
this myth is that very few of the people we love
are mind readers.  Regardless of how much
someone loves us, if we aren't willing to ask
for what we need, we're less likely to receive it.

When we accept responsibility for filling our
own needs we become less resentful or demanding
toward others.  As we learn to fill our own
needs we also become happier, more peaceful
and more unconditional in our relationships.

*How would you complete these phrases about needing?*

*Something I need that I could ask for is___*
*Taking responsibility for filling my own needs*
*helps me to feel___*

# Neediness

Neediness is what happens when we expect others to give us the support, affirmation and acceptance we have not yet given ourselves.

While each of us feels needy now and then, feeling too needy too often is a good indication that we aren't setting the kinds of limits that help us to care for ourselves.

*How would you complete these phrases relating to your own neediness?*

*A step I could take toward becoming less needy is____*
*A limit I could set that would help me to take better care of myself is____*

# Needs

While what we want may be optional, what we need is not. Ignoring our deep needs is a little like ignoring dandelions. The less we pay attention to them the more they color the landscape of our life.

Becoming more aware of our needs and assuming the responsibility for filling them, keeps us from manipulating others, and leads to more honest and loving relationships.

*How would you complete these phrases about needs?*

*One of my needs that I've been ignoring is____*
*A step I could take toward filling one of my needs is____*

# Negativity

Negativity for humans is like an oil spill for a bird. It traps us in a world that feels so unpleasant and harmful, that we can no longer live fully and our spirits lose their ability to fly.

Focusing on what is negative in our lives keeps us from taking steps toward what is positive.

Negativity is a habit. It's a way of seeing that diminishes our ability to live life with a sense of happiness and contentment. When we reduce the negativity in our lives our fears have fewer hooks on which to hang themselves.

---

*How would you complete these phrases about negativity?*

*One way my negative thinking affects my life is___*
*Looking for what is positive in my life helps me to___*
*A negative thought I could let go of is___*

## Niceness

How often, when we want something from
someone, do we disgust even ourselves with
our inauthentic niceness?

⌒⌒⌒⌒⌒⌒

*How would you complete this phrase about niceness?*

*When someone is overly nice to me I feel____*

## Not About Us

How others respond to us is usually colored by their own needs and beliefs.  How we respond to them is usually colored by our needs and beliefs as well.

Unless we are little children, we are rarely the center of someone else's universe.  When others are unkind to us or treat us disrespectfully, understanding that their words or actions are a reflection of their own lives can help us to respond more appropriately.

The more we see how little of life is really about us, the less we tend to take things personally and the happier and more positive we become.

*How would you complete these phrases about things that are not about you?*

*A belief that affects how I respond to others is____*
*Whenever I take things too personally*
*I notice that I also feel____*

# Noticing

The more we notice life's individual moments, the easier it becomes to direct those moments toward what fulfills and enriches us.

We need to teach ourselves to pause and observe our lives more fully. The more we notice, the more possibilities we are likely to see.

Our ability to change our lives in the future is based on our ability to notice how we are living in the present.

*How would you complete these phrases about noticing?*

*I could make this moment feel happier by___*
*A possibility I have just noticed is___*
*Something I am now doing that does not contribute to my overall happiness is___*

# Now

Now is the most powerful time for each of us. To love now, to laugh now, to take responsibility for our actions now, to make a difference now; these can be our constant and ongoing choices.

Since moments, once they've passed us by, are forever gone, we need to use them well. One of the best uses of this present moment is to make a decision to live life with greater awareness---beginning right now.

Our best response to life is to respond to what is now.

*How would you complete these phrases about now?*

*One positive thing I could do right now is___*
*I could live my life with a greater awareness by___*
*I could teach myself to be more present in the moment by___*

## *Personal Notes*

Needing_____

_____

_____

Neediness_____

_____

_____

Needs_____

_____

_____

Negativity_____

_____

_____

Niceness_____

_____

_____

Not About Us_____

_____

_____

Noticing_____

_____

_____

Now_____

_____

_____

*Opportunity, Optimism,*
*Feeling Overwhelmed*

# *Opportunity*

Perhaps our task in life is to recognize opportunity rather than to search for it.

The more fearful we feel about the unknown the less we are able to open the door to opportunities that are different than we imagined or expected.

When we believe our opportunities are limited, we live in a world of limitation. As we begin to see that opportunities are limitless, the boundaries of our worlds expand.

*How would you complete these phrases about opportunity?*

*An unexpected opportunity that once came to me was___*
*A fear that I could let go of is___*
*Some of the opportunities that already exist in my life are___*

# *O*

## *Optimism*

Cultivating an optimistic spirit is the result of choosing more positive thoughts more often.

We usually feel more inwardly powerful when we are optimistic. Optimism helps us to believe in greater possibility and purposefulness.

While pessimism has its roots in unreasonable fearfulness, optimism is rooted in reasonable hope. How much better our lives might be if we looked for more reasons to feel hopeful.

⋅⋏⋅⋅⋏⋅⋅⋏⋅⋅⋏⋅⋅⋏⋅

*How would you complete these phrases about optimism?*

*A positive thought I could choose for today is____*
*I could cultivate a more optimistic spirit by____*
*Some of my reasons for feeling hopeful are____*

# *Feeling Overwhelmed*

Feeling overwhelmed is the price we often pay for our unwillingness to ask for what we need.

Deciding to be a true participant in this dance of life is a powerful and freeing decision. It means we can choose the steps we wish to take. It also means we can choose not to dance at all if the music is not to our liking.

Imagine how much less overwhelmed we might feel if we began our day by subtracting just one task from our "to-do" list.

*How would you complete these phrases about feeling overwhelmed?*

*Something I need to ask for is____*
*Today I choose to____*
*One thing I don't need to do today is____*

## *Personal Notes*

Opportunity_____

_____

_____

Optimism_____

_____

_____

Feeling Overwhelmed_____

_____

_____

*Pain, Parenting, The Past,*
*The Path*
*Payment, Peace, Perception,*
*Perfection, Persistence,*
*Perspective, Pieces, The Plan,*
*Playfulness, Possibility,*
*Power From Within,*
*The Present, Priorities, Prison,*
*Procrastination, Progress,*
*Promises, Proving*

# Pain

We prolong our pain and create lasting scars when we focus on the ways that life has wounded us rather than on the ways we could heal ourselves from these emotional wounds.

While pain can sometimes be a good teacher, we were also created to learn from joy.

We seldom inflict pain on others without also injuring something within ourselves.

*How would you complete these phrases about pain?*

*A step I could take to begin to heal my emotional wounds is___*
*Something I learned from a happy experience was___*
*I hurt myself when___*

# Parenting

Children are our precious burdens. They are
the sacred fire that both warms and burns us.
To become a parent is to choose to walk toward
the ultimate unknown and all the unforeseen
responsibilities that can change our lives forever.

One of the truest tasks of parenting is to set
aside our fearfulness for our precious offspring
so they can live with greater courage for themselves.

Since feelings of perpetual guilt are part of the
parenting process, it is our constant task to
forgive ourselves for not having all the answers.
It is through this sense of self-acceptance and
compassion that we teach our children to honor
their own humanity.

*How would you complete these phrases about parenting?*

*Being a parent has helped me to____*
*I demonstrate my faith in my children by____*
*A guilty feeling I need to set aside is____*

# The Past

Respectfully remembering our pasts helps to keep us from repeating old mistakes. It also helps us to recognize the stepping stones that once led us to a greater sense of fulfillment.

When we drag the painful memories of our past into the present we feel fearful about our future. When we draw the successful memories from our past into the present we are able to see the future with more courage and more faith.

Seeing ourselves through more understanding, compassionate eyes helps us to learn from the parts of our pasts we may not remember with pride.

*How would you complete these phrases about the past?*

*Something in my past I remember respectfully is___*
*Some of my memories of success are___*
*I need to forgive myself for___*

# The Path

It's remarkable to notice how many positive as well as negative experiences have been placed on our path in order that we might have a fuller, richer life.

Sometimes the most important stepping stones on our path are disguised as stumbling blocks.

*How would you complete these phrases about the path?*

*A positive experience that was placed on my path was___*
*Something on my path*
*that was once disguised as a stumbling block is___*

# *Payment*

As long as we believe that hardship is the payment we must make for happiness, we'll always be afraid to be too happy for fear that the price may be too high.

What if the only payment we need to make for happiness is to acknowledge and to share it?

*How would you complete these phrases about payment?*

*Worrying about what may be potentially painful in life limits my ability to___*
*A sense of happiness that I need to share with someone is___*

# *Peace*

Peace, like joy, is something we consciously create within us. It is rarely something we accidentally stumble upon.


Peace at any price is almost always much too high a price to pay.


We enhance our sense of peacefulness by thinking compassionate, loving and empowering thoughts about ourselves as well as others.

*How would you complete these phrases about peace?*

*I could create more peacefulness within myself by____*
*I pay too high a price for peace when____*
*One of the compassionate, loving, empowering thoughts I could think about myself right now is____*

## *Perception*

Our pictures of life's possibilities are only
limited by the frames we put around them.

How we see even the smallest part of life is
usually an indication of how we see the rest of it.

*How would you complete these phrases about perception?*

*I could expand my perception of possibility by___*
*My usual way of looking at life is to ___*

# *Perfection*

What if our continual struggle for more perfection in life keeps us from noticing and appreciating the perfection that already exists?

Every time we shape ourselves to fit someone else's version of perfection we risk denying what is unique and perfect about who we already are.

What if we don't earn love by being perfect? What if it is our imperfection and our humanity that truly connects us to others?

* * *

*How would you complete these phrases about perfection?*

*Some of life's perfection that I can see today is___*
*When I try to fit myself into someone else's version*
*of perfection I notice that___*
*Accepting my own imperfections helps me to___*

# *Persistence*

Since persistence eventually wins, whenever we're persistent we improve our possibilities.

By combining persistence with flexibility, we enhance our potential for creating a fuller and more rewarding life.

As children we were persistent because we believed that anything was possible.  Perhaps as adults we need to re-awaken that belief in order to persist in creating a life that contains a greater sense of richness and contentment.

*How would you complete these phrases about persistence?*

*Something I was once persistent about was\_\_\_*
*I could be more flexible about\_\_\_*
*Believing that more in life is possible*
*would help me to become more persistent about\_\_\_*

## *Perspective*

All too often the perspective from which we view a problem, blocks our view of other possibilities.

While it doesn't really matter whether the toilet paper flows from above or below the roll, most of us habitually insert it the same way. One of the challenges in life is to look more closely at our habitual thoughts and actions so we can set aside those "toilet paper issues" that don't really contribute to the quality of our lives.

One of our responsibilities in life is to be as accepting as possible of other people's points of view, while continually re-examining our own.

*How would you complete these phrases about perspective?*

*I may be blocking my sense of possibility by____*
*One of my unimportant "toilet paper" issues is____*
*Another point of view I need to consider is____*

## *Pieces*

Even when an experience is difficult, there are usually pieces of that experience that come to us as gifts. The more we look for those pieces, the more we can use them to bring joy and purpose to our lives.

As we pay more attention to the way we live, we begin to notice that some of the pieces of our lives fill us with a sense of inner harmony, while others create a sense of inner discord. The clearer we become about the difference, the easier it becomes to choose between them.

*How would you complete these phrases about your life's pieces?*

*Something joyful that came to me*
*in the midst of a difficult experience was___*
*I notice that I create*
*more of a sense of harmony in my life when___*

## The Plan

Sometimes we don't recognize the gifts we receive in life because they come to us in unassembled pieces. It is by faithfully fitting those pieces together that the fullness of life's plan becomes become more evident  In the end, nothing we do or touch or experience in life is ever wasted or without meaning.

There is little of importance that we create or do alone. Each of us is a partner in the dance of life. As we listen for the melody and reach out to those around us we begin to see our steps in the dance more clearly. From within the deepest, truest part of us we begin to know that we are part of a universe that is much greater than ourselves.

*How would you complete these phrases about life's plan?*

*Something I've begun to notice about my life is____*
*Seeing my life as part of a greater plan helps me____*

# *Playfulness*

The spirit of playfulness is more precious than we can imagine.  It is the blessed seasoning that adds spontaneity and joyfulness to all we do in life.

Believing that playfulness is the opposite of work diminishes our ability for ongoing happiness. How much better our lives might be if we looked for opportunities to include a sense of playfulness within our daily tasks.

*How would you complete these phrases about playfulness?*

*I feel the most playful when___*
*I could add more of a sense of playfulness to what I am doing today by___*

# *Possibility*

Possibilities are like yellow cars.  The more we look for them the more we are likely to see.

The more willingly we look for possibilities the less we find to fear.

Imagine how our lives might change if we looked through the eyes of possibility.

*How would you complete these phrases about possibility?*

*Some of the possibilities in my life today are____*
*Feeling fearful limits my sense of possibility*
*as well as my ability to____*
*One thing I could do right now*
*to become more aware of life's possibilities is____*

## *Power From Within*

Real inner power frees us from the need to control our outer world. The key to this powerful freedom lies within our minds.

As we begin to let go of our need to exert power over others, our growing sense of self-containment releases us from their power over us.

We need to become more aware of our desire to control others by being too helpful, too giving or too sure we have the answers. The less we strive to exert this outer power the more inwardly powerful we become.

*How would you complete these phrases about inner power?*

*For me, feeling inwardly powerful means____*
*I feel more inwardly powerful when____*
*A part of life over which*
*I no longer need to exert outer power is____*

# *The Present*

Happiness lies in the present. Saying, "We'll be happy when…" guarantees we'll be less happy now.

Our present actions, attitudes and beliefs determine much of what we carry with us into the future

All of our power to create a fuller, richer life lies within the present. It is in the present that life's joy and power and possibility live most fully and completely.

*How would you complete these phrases about the present?*

*Something that contributes to my present happiness is___*
*Something I could change in the present that would help me to live more happily in the future is___*
*The more I focus on the present the more I notice that___*

# *Priorities*

Just as adding the proper seasoning enhances the flavor of food, setting good priorities adds fullness and richness to life.

The clearer we are about our priorities, the easier it becomes to let go of those things that do not contribute to the joy we find in life.

When our priorities are in line with what we value, it is easier to act on what is most essential for our sense of contentment and happiness.

*How would you complete these phrases about priorities?*

*One of my priorities for today is___*
*Something I'm trying to fit into my life*
*which is truly not a priority is___*
*Something I value that is reflected by my priorities is___*

# *Prison*

We need to be careful that the framework we
create for our lives doesn't become a cage that
limits and imprisons our full essence and potential.
The bars of our personal prisons are forged
from the limiting and outmoded beliefs we've
imposed upon ourselves.

*How would you complete this phrase about prison?*

*A belief that limits my happiness and keeps me from becoming
all that I can be is____*

# *Procrastination*

Procrastination rarely protects or empowers us. Waiting too long to remove a band-aid often delays the process of healing.

The longer we procrastinate the harder it becomes to take action.  It is the process of taking action that both frees and empowers us.

*How would you complete these phrases about procrastination?*

*Something I'm presently procrastinating about is___*
*An empowering action I could take today is___*

# *Progress*

Progress is not determined by the speed with which we walk or the length of our strides. Progress is simply the continual action of putting one foot in front of the other.

Sometimes progress doesn't seem to come from forward movement. Sometimes progress simply comes from not stopping too soon.

*How would you complete these phrases about progress?*

*I acknowledge myself for the progress I've already made in___*
*I could encourage myself to keep going by___*

# *Promises*

We are often better at keeping our promises to others than we are at keeping the ones we make to ourselves.

One of the most important parts of self-caring is to honor the promises that only we know we have made.

*How would you complete these phrases about promises?*

*One of the promises to myself that I need to keep is____*
*Some of the promises to myself that I have already kept are____*

# Proving

We need to give up our attempt to control an ever-widening sphere of the unnecessary. We need to give up feeling responsible for things that are out of our hands. We need to give up grabbing hold of new responsibilities just to prove we can handle them. It is much too exhausting to be continually proving ourselves to others. It is even more exhausting to be continually proving ourselves to ourselves.

*How would you complete this phrase about proving?*

*Something I no longer need to prove to myself is____*

# *Personal Notes*

Pain_____

_____

_____

Parenting_____

_____

_____

The Past_____

_____

_____

The Path_____

_____

_____

Payment_____

_____

_____

Peace_____

_____

_____

Perception_____

_____

_____

Perfection_____

_____

_____

# *Personal Notes*

Persistence_____

_____

_____

Perspective_____

_____

_____

Pieces_____

_____

_____

The Plan_____

_____

_____

Playfulness_____

_____

_____

Possibility_____

_____

_____

Power From Within_____

_____

_____

The Present_____

_____

_____

# *Personal Notes*

Priorities_____

_____

_____

Prison_____

_____

_____

Procrastination_____

_____

_____

Progress_____

_____

_____

Promises_____

_____

_____

Proving_____

_____

_____

*Quality, The Quest, Questions*

# Quality

The quality of our lives is built upon our definition of happiness and on our willingness to participate in creating it.

The quality of our lives is determined by how quickly we let go of those things that diminish our happiness so they don't impede us on our journeys.

*How would you complete these phrases about quality?*

*My definition of happiness is____*
*Something I need to let go of*
*that diminishes my happiness is____*

# The Quest

While having a dream opens the door to life's possibilities, it is our continuing quest for that dream that takes us through that door.

Our continuing quest for what fills our hearts most deeply adds value and meaning to every moment of our lives.

*How would you complete these phrases about your quest?*

*In my heart, what I want most deeply is____*
*One of the ways I stay true to my heart's desire is by____*

# Questions

The quality of life is often shaped by the kinds of questions we are willing to ask.

While making assumptions closes the door to true communication, asking questions helps us to keep that door open.

The more questions we ask the more understanding and compassionate we are likely to become.

*How would you complete these phrases about questions?*

*A question I need to ask myself is___*
*Someone I might understand more fully*
*if I asked them more questions is___*
*Being more understanding and compassionate*
*would also help me to___*

# Personal Notes

Quality_____

_____

_____

The Quest_____

_____

_____

Questions_____

_____

_____

*Reality, Receiving, Regrets,*
*Rejoicing, Relationships,*
*Rescuing, Resentment,*
*Responsibility, Risk, Rules, Ruts*

# *Reality*

What we believe determines our focus.  What
we focus on determines what is real for us in life.

Although what seems real in our minds is a fact
for us, we have the power to change our reality
by changing what we believe.

We cannot change anyone else's reality.  We
can only change our own.

*How would you complete these phrases about reality?*

*Some of what is real for me in my present life is___*
*A belief I may need to change*
*in order to change my reality is___*
*An action I could take that would improve my reality is___*

# Receiving

While it has been said that it is more blessed to give than it is to receive, conscious and grateful receivership blesses both the giver and the gift.

Keeping score diminishes the blessings of both giving and receiving.

As long as we believe that giving is synonymous with strength and receiving is synonymous with weakness, it will be difficult for us to receive from others with a grateful, open heart.

*How would you complete these phrases about receiving?*

*Someone who receives from me in a way that
helps me to feel good about myself is___
I need to stop keeping score about what
I give to and receive from___
I could make it more fun for others to give to me by___*

# Regrets

All too often our greatest regrets are for the times we didn't value ourselves or others enough. Taking reasonable responsibility for those regrets empowers us to live our lives with greater awareness.

Healthy regretting reminds us of our own humanity. Seeing ourselves through more generous, compassionate eyes helps us to see others that way as well.

Regrets alone can't change anything. What we do and who we become as a result of those regrets can change everything.

*How would you complete these phrases about regrets?*
*A regret that I acknowledge is____*
*A regret that has helped me*
*to become more compassionate is____*
*A regret about which I need to act more responsibly is____*

# R

## Rejoicing

Lovingly supporting others in their reasons for rejoicing is equally as important as supporting them in their suffering.

The more openly we share our reasons for rejoicing, the more we encourage others to celebrate their own.

We can change our lives, simply by becoming more aware of our own reasons for rejoicing.

*How would you complete these phrases about rejoicing?*

*Someone whose reasons for rejoicing*
*I need to support more fully is____*
*Someone with whom I need to share*
*my own reasons for rejoicing is____*
*Some of the reasons I have for rejoicing are____*

# Relationships

Healthy relationships with others are rooted in the healthy relationship we have with ourselves.

Since being defensive gets in the way of relationships, the clearer we are about our own self-worth the better our relationships are likely to be.

We have two clear choices about what to do with the stones we discover on life's path. We can use them to build walls that protect us from others, or we can use them to create pathways that lead toward more accepting, supportive relationships.

*How would you complete these phrases about relationships?*

*One of the ways I honor*
*the relationship I have with myself is____*
*When I am responding defensively I notice that____*
*I could build a better path toward*
*more supportive, accepting relationships by____*

# Rescuing

We need to beware of that rescuer part of ourselves that takes over people's lives, by trying to anticipate what is best for them through the limited vantage point of we think we know.

The more we believe in the inner strength of others, the less we need to rescue them and the more we empower them to care for themselves.

*How would you complete these phrases about rescuing?*

*I feel the most tempted to rescue others when___*
*Someone I could empower through my belief in them is___*

# Resentment

Resentment is something that is apt to be more present in our lives when we don't acknowledge and respond honestly to our own feelings.

The more honest we are about our resentments the more it becomes possible to resolve them.

Remembering that what happens in life is rarely personal can help us to avoid feeling resentful.

*How would you complete these phrases about resentment?*

*Something I feel resentful about is____*
*A step I could take*
*toward healing one of my resentments is____*
*Something I am presently taking too personally is____*

# Responsibility

While accepting responsibility for our actions empowers and enriches us, refusing to accept responsibility causes us to feel victimized and powerless.

When we avoid personal responsibility by making excuses or blaming others, we risk losing our ability to influence the direction of our lives.

The more self-valuing we become, the more naturally we accept personal responsibility.

*How would you complete these phrases about responsibility?*

*I need to assume more responsibility for___*
*When I use my energy for blaming or for making excuses I notice that___*
*One positive result of my taking greater personal responsibility is___*

# R

## *Risk*

Ultimately those who are willing to take ongoing reasonable risks live their lives with less fear and with a more fulfilling sense of what is possible.

In order to grow more, we need to be willing to risk more.

Risking just a little every day helps us to crack open the soil of our lives so new seeds of fulfillment and happiness will have the opportunity to grow. Over time, stretching ourselves to feel just a little uncomfortable expands our sense of what feels possible and safe.

*How would you complete these phrases about risk?*

*A positive result from a risk I have taken is___*
*A place in my life*
*where I need to risk a little more is___*
*A small risk I could take today is___*

## Rules

We need to teach ourselves to constantly question the rules for living that we have created for our lives.

When we live with a sense of respectfulness toward ourselves and others, the rules for living that are most meaningful become a more natural part of our lives.

*How would you complete these phrases about rules?*

*One of my rules for living that I need to question is____*
*One of my rules for living*
*that still feels comfortable and helpful is____*

# Ruts

Whenever we're clinging too tightly to our pictures of how our lives should look, we slip into a rut that keeps us from seeing the value and importance of being willing to change and grow.

While following the accepted ruts of life may seem to keep us safe, it robs us of the adventure of exploring what is possible.

⌁⌁⌁⌁⌁

*How would you complete these phrases about ruts?*

*I feel as though I am in a rut about___*
*A step I could make*
*toward moving out of one of my ruts is___*

# *R*

## *Personal Notes*

Reality_____
_____
_____

Receiving_____
_____
_____

Regrets_____
_____
_____

Rejoicing_____
_____
_____

Relationships_____
_____
_____

Rescuing_____
_____
_____

Resentment_____
_____
_____

## *Personal Notes*

Responsibility_____

_____

_____

Risk_____

_____

_____

Rules_____

_____

_____

Ruts_____

_____

_____

*Safety, The Secret,*
*Seeds, Self-Absorption, Self-Appreciation,*
*Self-Awareness, Self-Caring,*
*Self-Celebration, Self-Empowerment,*
*Self-Gratitude, Selfishness, Self-Knowing,*
*Self-Love, Self-Protection, Self-Worth,*
*Stress, Struggle, Success,*
*Supporting Others, Survivorship*

## *Safety*

Assuming reasonable responsibility for our
own physical and emotional safety helps us to
live with more confidence and faith.

Setting the kinds of limits that keep our spirits
safe is easier and more natural when we are
listening to our instincts and staying truthful
to ourselves.

*How would you complete these phrases about safety?*

*One of the ways I assume responsibility
for my physical safety is by___*
*One of the ways I contribute to my emotional safety is by___*

## *The Secret*

The secret to living more fulfilling lives is to do the best we can every day.

The secret to living with a more contented, peaceful spirit is to remember that we are rarely the center of any one else's universe and very little in life is truly directed toward us.

The secret to living a happier, more powerful life is to keep our energy in the present and to be continually aware of our reasons for feeling compassionate and grateful.

*How would you complete these phrases relating to the secret?*

*One thing I could do better today is___*
*Something I don't need to take so personally is___*
*Something I could do to keep my energy in the present is___*

## Seeds

The seeds of our tomorrows are planted in today.

Once we have planted the seeds for our tomorrows, we need to water them and care for them, faithfully resisting the temptation to dig them up to see if they are growing.

*How would you complete these phrases about seeds?*

*Something I could do today
that would positively affect a part of my future is___
I care for the seeds I have already planted in my life by___*

# Self-Absorption

If everything in life seems somehow to be about us, chances are we're overly self-absorbed. When we're too busy noticing how others are responding to us, we're probably not listening very well to them.

We risk causing others to think their feelings are unimportant or insignificant when we are too involved with the importance of our own.

The more we focus on how others feel about themselves the less we are likely to focus on how they feel about us.

* * *

*How would you complete these phrases about self absorption?*

*I could improve my ability to listen by___*
*When I'm too involved with my own feelings I notice that___*
*Someone who needs me to help them*
*feel better about themselves is___*

# Self-Appreciation

What if we could change our lives by creating an ongoing list of what we appreciate in ourselves?

The more we acknowledge and appreciate the positive parts of ourselves, the more centered and confident we become.

The more we like and appreciate ourselves, the less we need to work to get others to like us.

*How would you complete this phrase about self appreciation?*

*Some of the things I appreciate about myself are___*
*Feeling more self-confident helps me to___*
*Working too hard to get others to like me leaves me feeling___*

# Self-Awareness

True self-awareness lies in our ability to acknowledge both the dark and the sunlit parts of who we really are.

A healthy sense of self-awareness helps us to build upon the parts of our lives that are expansive and empowering. It also helps us to honor and heal the parts of our lives that keep us from living with enough confidence and faith.

*How would you complete these phrases about self awareness?*

*Some of the sunlit parts of who I am are___*
*A part of my life that I need to heal is___*

# Self-Caring

While true self-caring sometimes comes from the visible things we do for ourselves, it also comes from the compassionate, life-affirming, invisible thoughts we think about ourselves.

Building a respectful relationship with ourselves is the core of true self-caring. It keeps us from giving too much to others with the fragile hope that they will somehow be able to replenish us in return.

Setting good limits is a kind of self caring that protects us from entering into relationships that do not nurture or sustain us.

*How would you complete these phrases about self caring?*

*A kindly thought I could think about myself is____*
*When I stop myself from giving too much to others*
*I notice that____*
*A limit I truly need to set is____*

# Self-Celebration

Since self-celebration has its roots in the past,
we need to send ourselves a little confetti now
and then to celebrate how far we've already come.

When we consistently acknowledge and celebrate
our small successes, we feel less discouraged
when we disappoint ourselves.

The more we are able to see and celebrate the
positive parts of who we are, the more natural
it becomes to see and celebrate the positive parts
of others.

*How would you complete these phrases about self celebration?*

*Some of my past successes are\_\_\_\_*
*One of the ways in which I am successful now is\_\_\_\_*
*Some of the positive parts of others*
*that I also celebrate in myself are\_\_\_\_*

# Self-Empowerment

It's usually more empowering to be a "pain"
than it is to be a pushover.

Every time we acknowledge our strengths or
affirm our positive attributes and every time
we remember our past successes or encourage
ourselves to keep trying, we empower ourselves
and add more possibility and purpose to our lives.

Sometimes we need to decrease our discomfort
with how others see us so we can increase our
comfort with how we see ourselves.

⸰⸏⸰⸏⸰⸏⸰⸏⸰⸏⸰

*How would you complete these phrases about self
empowerment?*

*I'm too much of a pushover about____*
*One of my strengths that helps to empower me is____*
*Someone else's perception of me
that diminishes my faith in myself is____*

# Self-Gratitude

Feeling grateful for who we are, is an essential part of living fuller and more rewarding lives.

Feeling grateful for who we are helps us to honor our own worth.  Honoring our own worth empowers us to set better boundaries for how we allow other to treat us.

The magical thing about self-gratitude is that it builds self-confidence.

*How would you complete this phrase about self gratitude?*

*Some of the parts of myself for which I feel grateful are____*
*A place in my life where I need to set better boundaries is____*
*I feel self-confident about____*

# Selfishness

While unhealthy selfishness keeps us from
respecting the needs of others, healthy
selfishness helps us to respect and honor
our own.

Being selfish enough to take care of our own
needs keeps us from self-centeredly manipulating
others into filling them for us. Being selfish
enough to take care of our own needs actually
frees us to become more present for others.

If it is selfish to consider our own needs and to
be responsible for taking care of them, perhaps
we need to be more selfish more often.

*How would you complete these phrases about selfishness?*

*One of my needs that I could honor more fully is___*
*When I manipulate others into filling my needs*
*I notice that___*
*Seeing the positive side of selfishness helps me to___*

# Self-Knowing

It's important not to let our focus on what we do diminish our knowledge of who we are.

As long as we view ourselves through the eyes of others, our self-knowing will be colored by someone else's values and beliefs.

True self-knowing helps us to make better choices and to stay more balanced in the midst of life's challenges.

*How would you complete these phrases about self knowing?*

*I know myself to be the kind of person who____*
*I see myself through my own eyes more easily when____*
*I have made good choices about____*

# *Self-Love*

Sometimes when we are looking too hard for someone else to love us, we forget that the most healing and empowering kind of loving begins within ourselves.

Healthy self-loving helps us to make choices based on what is good for us and true to what we value. Healthy self-loving helps to keep us from feeling resentful or unappreciated.

The more we treat ourselves with love and compassion, the more natural it becomes to expect the same treatment from others. If we don't genuinely love ourselves, we're committed to becoming perpetual actors in order to manipulate those around us to do our loving for us.

*How would you complete these phrases about self love?*

*I could become more loving toward myself by___*
*When I treat myself lovingly I notice that___*

# Self-Protection

It is easier to celebrate what is precious in our lives when we are not distracted by our fear of losing it.

Since we can't hold onto anything of value with a clenched fist, we need to maintain an ongoing balance between vulnerability and self-protection.

One of the most powerful forms of self-protection is the stand we take against negativity.

*How would you complete these phrases about self protection?*

*Some of the precious things I celebrate in life are____*
*Someone with whom I can be vulnerable is____*
*Something I could do to protect myself from negativity is____*

# Self-Worth

Self-worth is rooted in self-acknowledgement. The more we focus on the positive parts of who we are and what we do, the more our sense of personal worthiness empowers us.

Whenever we're feeling angry or resentful for not being valued by others, we need to look more closely at how well we are valuing ourselves. The clearer we become about our own self-worth, the less likely we are to attract relationships that are lacking in respectfulness.

*How would you complete these phrases about self-worth?*

*I acknowledge myself to be someone who can____*
*One of my relationships that affirms my self-worth is____*

## *Stress*

Sometimes we contribute to the stress in our lives by taking on something new just when we're almost caught up.

If our definition of a good day is simply a day with less stress, we need to look more closely at our choices. When our choices are based on what we truly value, our days become more satisfying and comfortable.

Much of the stress that is present in our lives comes not from doing too much, but from doing too little of what we truly enjoy.

*How would you complete these phrases about stress?*

*Something I can take off my to-do list for today is____*
*A choice I need to make*
*that is more in line with what I value is____*
*Some of the things I truly enjoy are____*

# *Struggle*

The more we believe in struggle the less we are likely to experience effortlessness.

Believing we must cause or force a specific outcome increases the sense of struggle in our lives. Seeking instead to participate in finding a positive outcome increases our sense of ease and possibility.

When our lives feel too filled with struggle, we need to look more closely at our focus. When we shift or broaden our focus we increase our awareness of effortlessness and possibility.

⋅⌃⋅ ⋅⌃⋅ ⋅⌃⋅ ⋅⌃⋅ ⋅⌃⋅

*How would you complete these phrases about struggle?*

*A place in my life that feels effortless today is____*
*Looking for possibilities helps me to____*
*I need to shift or broaden my focus about____*

# *Success*

Success is not simply a final result.  Success is an ongoing process built on small steady steps, all heading in the same direction.

While some of our dreams may lie in the future, being continually aware of our daily successes helps to fulfill and empower us in the present.

Living a life that is true to what we value is the most powerful and meaningful measure of success.

*How would you complete these phrases about success?*

*Some of the small steps I am presently taking
toward my eventual success are___
Something I feel successful about today is___
For me, living successfully means___*

# *Supporting Others*

Listening with an open and compassionate
heart is much more supportive than giving advice.

Because we hold up the mirror in which others
often see themselves, it is important that the
reflection we create is as positive and powerful
as possible.

Living our own lives with the belief that
anything is possible helps us to become more
supportive of others.

*How would you complete these phrases about s
upporting others?*

*When I keep myself from giving unsolicited advice
I notice____*
*Someone for whom I could
hold up a more positive and powerful mirror is____*
*If I truly believed in limitless possibility I would____*

## *Survivorship*

While it is appropriate to celebrate those times we've survived the hard and sometimes tragic parts of life, the real celebration begins when we move beyond that basic survivorship to the place where we acknowledge and celebrate our ability to thrive.

*How would you complete this phrase about survivorship?*

*A place in my life I am already thriving is___*

# *Personal Notes*

Safety_____

_____

_____

The Secret_____

_____

_____

Seeds_____

_____

_____

Self-Absorption_____

_____

_____

Self-Appreciation_____

_____

_____

Self-Awareness_____

_____

_____

Self-Caring_____

_____

_____

# *Personal Notes*

Self-Celebration_____

_____

_____

Self-Empowerment_____

_____

_____

Self-Gratitude_____

_____

_____

Selfishnes_____

_____

_____

Self-Knowing_____

_____

_____

Self-Love_____

_____

_____

Self Protection_____

_____

_____

# *Personal Notes*

Self-Worth_____

_____

_____

Stress_____

_____

_____

Struggle_____

_____

_____

Success_____

_____

_____

Supporting Others_____

_____

_____

Survivorship_____

_____

_____

*Time, Today,*
*Trust, Truth*

# Time

Time, if we let it, can touch the edges of our memory with a kindly sort of mist that offers us a deeper sense of understanding and compassion.

If there is never quite enough time to accomplish all the things on our to-do lists, chances are we're confusing what we want to do with what we truly need to do.

Time is a precious gift that is given equally to each of us. We can waste it with procrastination, anger and laziness or we can fill it with what we love and value. Ultimately, the way we consciously receive this precious gift determines the meaningfulness and the quality of our lives.

*How would you complete these phrases about time?*

*A difficult time in my life that I now see differently is___*
*Something I don't truly need to do today is___*
*Today I could use my time more positively by___*

# Today

Today is the most powerful time we have. To live today with as much awareness and truthfulness and positive energy as we can, is to build a powerful and healing path toward tomorrow.

Today is the day to remember the blessings in our lives and to use them to expand our sense of possibility.

*How would you complete these phrases about today?*

*Today I will use my positive energy for___*
*Today I feel especially grateful for___*

# Trust

There is a time after we have done what we
can do, when we must simply step back and trust.
It is that time between the planting and the
harvest, when we need to simply need to believe
that the seeds we have planted are growing.

How many times do we ask directions, only to
discover that we're already on the right road?
Sometimes we simply need to trust ourselves
just to go a little farther.

*How would you complete these phrases about trust?*

*A place in my life that I need to be more trusting is____*
*A place in my life that I could trust myself to go a little*
*farther is____*

# Truth

Becoming more truthful with ourselves is an important first step in becoming more truthful with others.

While the truth can sometimes feel uncomfortable, telling that truth with kindness and compassion ultimately sets us free.

When we only speak a part of the truth it can often become the only part we see.

*How would you complete these phrases about truth?*

*Something in my life that I would change*
*if I were more truthful to myself is___*
*Someone to whom I need to tell the truth is___*
*I need to tell myself the whole truth about___*

## *Personal Notes*

Time_____

_____

_____

Today_____

_____

_____

Trust_____

_____

_____

Truth_____

_____

_____

*Understanding, Uniqueness,*
*Feeling Useful, Using*
*What We Have*

# Understanding

We diminish our potential for happiness when we over-analyze life. Life is an unfolding mystery, not simply a problem to be solved.

Sometimes as we seek to understand others, we discover something in them that gives us a deeper understanding of ourselves.

Sometimes it's not nearly as important that we understand those we love as it is that we accept and believe in them.

*How would you complete these phrases about understanding?*

*A part of my life that I could analyze less is ___*
*Someone in whom I see a part of myself is___*
*Someone I need to accept more fully right now is___*

# Uniqueness

While each of us is truly unique, we also drink from the universal stream of hopes, fears, dreams and disappointments which are common to us all. Becoming more aware of our similarities helps us to build a deeper sense of connection between ourselves and others.

As we seek to recognize our uniqueness in the midst of our deep connection to others, our lives become more purposeful and peaceful.

The courage it takes to express our own uniqueness helps us to become more of what we were so lovingly created to be.

⸱⌄⸱⌄⸱⌄⸱⌄⸱⌄⸱

*How would you complete these phrases about uniqueness?*

*Some of the ways I am similar to others are___*
*A part of myself that is unique is___*
*I believe I was created to be___*

# Feeling Useful

The need to contribute and to be of service lies deep within each of us. Feeling useful and therefore, valuable, is an essential part of living a rich and meaningful life.

One of the most powerful forms of usefulness is our willingness to listen with a quiet and compassionate heart.

What if, in our headlong rush to be useful, we forget to ask others whether what we want to give them is what they want to receive?

*How would you complete these phrases about usefulness?*

*Someone I need to thank*
*for their contribution to my life is___*
*Someone who simply needs me to listen is___*
*Someone to whom I may give inappropriately is___*

## Using What We Have

We need to be more aware of what we already have in our lives if we are to use it more meaningfully.

Often, when we are busily looking for more, we forget to notice and build upon what we already have.

*How would you complete these phrases about using what you already have?*

*One of my positive qualities
that I could develop more fully is___
Something I already have
that I need to notice how I'm using is___*

# *Personal Notes*

Understanding_____

_____

_____

Uniqueness_____

_____

_____

Feeling Useful_____

_____

_____

Using What We Have_____

_____

_____

*Values, Vantage Point, Velcro®*
*Being A Victim, Vision, Vulnerability*

# Values

The greater the disparity between what we do
and what we say we value, the more overwhelmed
and unhappy we are likely to be.

The clearer we are about what we value, the
easier it becomes to make the kinds of choices
that help us to live a fuller and happier life.

*How would you complete these phrases about values?*

*Some of the things I value are____*
*A choice I need to make*
*that is more in line with what I value is____*

# *Vantage Point*

Our vantage point is partially determined by
past memories and experiences.  It is also
determined by what we choose to see in the present.


Since much of what we see in life is determined
by what we are looking for, sometimes the vantage
point from which we see a problem limits our
ability to solve it.


If what we believe and how we behave grow
from habit rather than from conscious choice,
it may be time to look more closely at our
vantage point.

· ⌃ · ⌃ · ⌃ · ⌃ · ⌃ ·

*How would you complete these phrases about vantage point?*

*Something in my life that I once saw differently is____*
*A time when the way I looked at a problem*
*made it hard for me to solve it was____*
*I could choose a more positive vantage point by____*

# *Velcro*®

Learning to take things less personally is like learning to take off a jacket made of Velcro®. As we see how little of life is truly about us, our unpleasant past experiences are less likely to cling to us and weigh us down.

The less Velcro® we wear, the freer we become to do life's dance with a sense of joyful gratitude and love.

*How would you complete these phrases about Velcro®?*

*A place in my life
where I can see that I'm wearing Velcro® is___
I could remind myself to remove my Velcro® by___*

## *Being A Victim*

The more we blame how we feel or behave on
something outside us the more we see ourselves
as victims. Taking the responsibility for learning
to swim makes us much less likely to be tossed
by life's waves.

The angrier and more blaming we feel, the
more we need to look at how we've contributed
to our roles as victims.

When we are setting ourselves up for someone
to take advantage of us, it's helpful to remember
that being a victim never improves the quality
of our lives.

*How would you complete these phrases about being a victim?*

*I could take more responsibility about___*
*Someone with whom I've allowed myself to be a victim is___*
*When I feel like a victim I also notice that___*

## Vision

There is a clear relationship between how we see ourselves and what we are able to do in our lives.

Having a vision for greater possibility enhances the quality of our lives.

*How would you complete these phrases about vision?*

*I see myself as someone who can____*
*Part of my vision for what is possible is____*

# *Vulnerability*

While weakness may be rooted in fearfulness, vulnerability is built on the courage it takes to become more personally honest.

Vulnerability is essential to honest relationships. It is a symbol of our authenticity, our values and our willingness to walk in the light of who we truly are.

*How would you complete these phrases about vulnerability?*

*When I am vulnerable enough
to be personally honest I notice____
One of the ways I could help others to feel safe enough to be
vulnerable with me is____*

# *Personal Notes*

Values_____

_____

_____

Vantage Point_____

_____

_____

Velcro®_____

_____

_____

Being A Victim_____

_____

_____

Vision_____

_____

_____

Vulnerability_____

_____

_____

*Wholeness, Wisdom, Wishing*
*Wonder, Work, Writing*

## *Wholeness*

To be whole is to choose to stand in that
nonjudgmental part of ourselves that allows
and loves all things as a part of something
greater and more mysterious than our minds
can comprehend.

One of the secrets to living a more contented
life is to notice and savor those moments when
we feel the gift of wholeness within us.

Very little in life is truly consistent. Days are
made of mornings and evenings, darkness and
light. We need to remember this when we're
judging ourselves for not being as whole or
consistent as we would truly like to be.

*How would you complete these phrases about wholeness?*

*I could become less judgmental of others by___*
*I feel the gift of wholeness within me when___*
*I show greater acceptance toward myself when___*

# *Wisdom*

Each of us was created with a wise and loving heart. It is that part of us that honors life as it comes to us and sees the best within it.

We are more likely to be touched and guided by our inner wisdom when we are listening rather than talking.

It is easier to put our inner wisdom to work for us when we are focusing on what is good and positive in our lives.

⋅⋏⋅⋅⋏⋅⋅⋏⋅⋅⋏⋅⋅⋏⋅

*How would you complete these phrases about wisdom?*

*Someone I know whose heart is wise and loving is____*
*Something I once realized while I was listening was____*
*I could focus more consistently on what is positive and good in my life by____*

# Wishing

The most empowering part of making any
wish is to connect it to an action that can help
it to come true.

Whenever we wish that time would pass more
quickly we risk losing the opportunity for filling
that time with something that could help us
build a fuller, richer life.

⚬⚬⚬⚬⚬

*How would you complete these phrases about wishing?*

*A step I could take
toward making one of my wishes come true is___
One of the ways I could use my time to build a richer life is___*

# Wonder

Wonder opens doors to possibility in a way that assuming rarely does.

A sense of wonder expands that part of us that is curious and believes in possibility. It enlivens our spirits and enriches our lives.

The more we think we know, the less we are likely to wonder.

*How would you complete these phrases about wonder?*

*A possibility I have wondered about is____*
*The last time I felt a sense of wonder was____*
*A way I could include*
*a greater sense of wonder in my life is to____*

## Work

If it doesn't get done today, maybe it's not important.

Setting arbitrary deadlines causes us to focus fearfully on the future and keeps us from living more joyfully in the present.

Why do we often think of work as negative when it provides for our sustenance, offers us a place to use our talents and gives us an opportunity to serve? There is only one letter's difference between the words "joy" and "job". Perhaps our challenge is to weave a sense of joyfulness into this thing we call work, so we can think about it more positively

·▲· ·▲· ·▲· ·▲· ·▲·

*How would you complete these phrases about work?*

*Something I don't really need to do today is\_\_\_*
*One of my arbitrary deadlines is\_\_\_*
*One of the positive things my work gives me is\_\_\_*

# Writing

One of the most important ways to nurture and heal our spirit is to write. There is something about committing our thoughts and feelings to paper that helps us to discover and use what is truly inside us. The simple act of writing helps us to put handles on our inner drawers, especially the ones that seem to be stuck.

To write is to take a journey of self-discovery. It helps us to follow our dreams and to focus on what is important for our lives. It also helps us to find more compassion within us for the star-bright, yet sometimes tarnished person whom we know ourselves to be.

*How would you complete these thoughts about writing?*

*A consistent time of the day when I could write is____*
*A feeling I need to write about is____*

## *Personal Notes*

Wholeness_____

_____

_____

Wisdom_____

_____

_____

Wishing_____

_____

_____

Wonder_____

_____

_____

Work_____

_____

_____

Writing_____

_____

_____

*X Marks The Spot, Being 'Xactly*
*Where We Need To Be*
*Yes, Yet, Zest,*

# X Marks The Spot

In treasure maps, X marks the spot at the end of the journey where the treasure is hidden. In life, X marks our turning points and the experiences that have helped us to grow and to change.

The true treasure in life lies in our ability to love ourselves and others more unconditionally. The true treasure lies in our ability to wonder, to seek possibility, to laugh and to be aware of our blessings. The true treasure in life lies in our ability to grieve and feel sorrowful, then to grow and heal and find new nourishment for our souls.

The more we notice life's true treasures the more mental X's we have on our personal treasure map.

*How would you complete these phrases about X marks the spot?*

*One of my turning points was___*
*Some of my life's true treasures are___*

# Being 'Xactly Where
# We Need To Be

What if we truly believed that where we are right now is exactly the place we are supposed to be? What if we spent less energy and effort struggling to change our place in life? What if we simply looked at where we're standing and opened our eyes a little wider? What might we notice? What might we discover? What might we wonder about? What might we learn? How might we grow? The important changes in life seldom come from an experience itself. They come from the way we see that experience and from the way we respond to what we see.

*How would you complete this phrase about being 'xactly where you need to be?*

*I am 'xactly in the right place in my life to____*

# *Y*

## *Yes*

It's interesting how often life supports our beliefs. If we believe that an experience will be difficult, life often says, "Yes, you are right," then shows us that it is so. If instead we believe that we can live with greater peace and happiness, life usually says "yes" to that then helps us find the way.

When we hold out our arms and say "yes" to life we open ourselves to receive more of its gifts.

When we hold out our arms and say "yes" to too many tasks and obligations we limit our ability to receive life's gifts because our arms are already too full.

*How would you complete these phrases about yes?*

*Life recently said "yes" to me about____*
*Something I can choose not to say "yes" to today is____*

## *Yet*

"Yet" is an interesting little word. Used at the end of a sentence it can change a sense of failure into a sense of possibility. When we think that we have not reached our dreams we are likely to feel sad and hopeless. When we tell ourselves we haven't reached them yet...we leave room for possibility.

* · · · · · · · · · · · · · · · · · ·

*How would you complete this phrase about "yet"?*

*Something I'm willing to work for
that isn't a part of my life yet is____*

## Zest

We feel the most zest for life when we are doing what gives us the greatest happiness. The secret to living a more zestful life is to do more of those things more often.

·⌒·⌒·⌒·⌒·⌒·

*How would you complete this phrase about zest?*

*Something I want to do more of in my life is___*

## *Personal Notes*

X Marks the Spot_____

_____

_____

Being 'Xactly Where We Need To Be_____

_____

_____

Yes_____

_____

_____

Yet_____

_____

_____

Zest_____

_____

_____

# Grateful Acknowledgments

*No book is ever written without enormous help, love and support from others. While the list of those who have traveled with me on this journey is endless, there are four people whom I would especially like to acknowledge.*

## Parker Babbidge
*Parker is the unique and amazing man with whom I share both my life and my dreams. A former jazz musician, actor and world traveler, Parker now alternates writing screenplays with the 32 foot classic wooden sail boat he is building in our back yard. He has an insatiable appetite for both learning and life and a sense of humor that nearly always makes me smile. Parker has lovingly supported me in this sometimes solitary journey of writing. He edits, cooks, listens and loves me unconditionally. Thank you, Parker, for the true blessing of your presence in my life.*

## Carole Rako
*Carole is a clinical social worker with a thriving psychotherapy practice in Norfolk, Massachusetts, where she is well known for her wise and healing approach to personal challenges. She is a great cook and a smart, funny, insightful and compassionate woman. She is also my dear and trusted friend. Carole sat with me as we reviewed each of these thoughts and questions, helping me to make them more meaningful and clear. Thank you, Carole, for the way you touched the pages of this book with your healing, generous and empowering spirit.*

## Lesley Avery Gould

Lesley Avery Gould is a multifaceted, wonder-filled and courageously independent woman. She is also my sister and my friend. Lesley explores the underwater world as a videographer and feature film editor. Her unique talent for reflecting the mystery and majesty of life, both above and below the water, has won her international recognition. Lesley, who illustrated my first book, guided me in combining the visual ingredients for this collection of thoughts. Thank you, Lesley, for the countless ways you have supported me in following my dreams.

## Kimberli Norton

Kim is my dear and precious daughter, the mother of two of my grandchildren and the president of Treasured Photographs. She is a gifted children's photographer whose innate ability to capture the true essence and magical spirit of her subjects makes her work heart-stoppingly tangible and tender. Thank you, Kim, for your blessed and unrepeatable presence in my life and for the photos of me that appear in this book.

## I would also like to thank:

My mother, Catherine Heustis, who looked for the creative gifts in each of her children, then encouraged us to use them. I am grateful to my loving and life-embracing son Ken, who is such a great father to my other two grandchildren, and to Christine Zimmer, Mary Dillinger and Bruce Heustis, my sisters and brother, all of whom have loved and believed in me throughout my years of writing.

Debbie Yeoh is the person I've turned to when I was feeling discouraged. Thank you, Debbie, for your incredible heart and

*for the way you have always helped me to maintain my courage and my faith. Pat Hardy manages my design firm. She is also my very special friend. Thank you, Pat, for taking on more than your share so I could write and for the honest and compassionate way in which you listen.*

*Julia Perce helped me to edit both my thoughts and my words. David Milley and Sandra McCrary from Accent Press in Dedham Massachusetts took personal care of the graphics and made the production of this book both effortless and fun. These three talented and dedicated, people have truly partnered with me to bring this book to you.*

*I'm thankful to my countless friends, for consistently encouraging and believing in me. I'm thankful to the people I may never meet, who read my first book, then shared it. I'm thankful, too, for those of you who heard my motivational storytelling, and told your friends about me. My heart is full and my blessing are many.*

*My last and most important wish is to thank our Creator, who is the true author of this book.*

# About Gail Van Kleeck

*Gail Van Kleeck is a mother, a grandmother, an international inspirational author and a motivational storyteller. She is also an interior design consultant and the president of Dover Interiors, a design firm that specializes in helping its clients create surroundings that nurture their spirits.*

*Gail spent seven years as a Hospice volunteer. Her writing and speaking contain insights drawn from the families with whom she was privileged to work. She also draws from her childhood experiences, her journals and her life as a daughter, wife, mother and friend.*

Gail's first internationally published book, **How You See Anything Is How You See Everything**. is a collection of simple, inspirational stories that demonstrate how a difference in our focus can make a difference in our lives. The model of persistence, it took her twenty-five years and more than a hundred rejections to find a publisher for that book.

The oldest of five children, Gail grew up in Michigan. She and her life's partner, Parker Babbidge, now live in a small cottage in Westwood, Massachusetts, a suburb of Boston, where they enjoy their friends and family and where there is also a tent and a fire-pit in the back yard for camping out with grandchildren.

Gail would be most grateful if you would send your friends to her website. She believes that as we expand our personal sense of fulfillment and happiness we also become a powerful force for the healing that is so badly needed in our sometimes troubled world.

You can contact Gail through her website, www.simplewisdom.com

# Other Books by Gail Van Kleeck

*How You See Anything Is How You See Everything* is a collection of simple, insightful stories that demonstrate how a difference in our focus can make a difference in our lives. It was endorsed by John Gray, author of Men Are From Mars, Women Are From Venus and translated into Mandarin for publication in China. While this wise little book is easy to read, the gentle yet powerful message of its stories is difficult to forget.

**A Home With A Heart** is an approachable, inspirational, practical decorating guide for creating a welcoming, spirit-nurturing home. Playfully illustrated by Gail's sister, Lesley Avery Gould, A Home With A Heart helps to replace the fear that is often a part of decorating with a sense of confidence and fun. Gail draws on her more than 30 years as an interior design consultant as she completes this unique and helpful book. Look for news of its upcoming release on her website.

The website address is **www.simplewisdom.com**

# QUICK ORDER FORM

Phone orders:    781-255-0808
Fax orders:      copy this form and fax to 781-762-3068
Email orders:    www.simplewisdom.com
Postal orders:   Abundance Enterprises,
                 PO Box 201.  Westwood, Ma. 02090

*Please send me information about motivational storytelling/seminars*____
*Please email me your Simple Wisdom Newsletter*____

Please send me the following books

|  | Quantity | Total |
|---|---|---|
| *Simple Wisdom for Challenging* Times ..$16.95 per copy | ____ | _____ |
| *How You See Anything is How You See Everything*...$12.95 per copy | ____ | _____ |

Please add $3.50 shipping and handling per copy to your total.
Massachusetts residents also need to add 5% tax per copy

Total Cost of Books_____5% Ma. Resident tax_____

Total Cost of Handling_____Total Payment_____

Name_____

Address_____

City_____State_____Zip_____

Telephone_____email_____

Method of Payment    check_____

                     Visa_____          Mastercard____

Card number_____

Name on Card_____

Expiration Date_____